This Independent Republic

Studies in the Nature and Meaning of American History

Rousas John Rushdoony

ROSS
HOUSE
BOOKS

Vallecito, California

Copyright 1964
Dorothy Rushdoony
and the Rushdoony irrevocable trust

reprinted 2001

Ross House Books
PO Box 67
Vallecito, CA 95251
www.rosshousebooks.org

All rights reserved.

No part of this book may be reproduced, stored in a retrieval
system, or transmitted in any form or by any means — electronic,
mechanical, photocopy, recording, or otherwise — except for brief
quotations for the purpose of review or comment, without the
prior written permission of the publisher.

Library of Congress Control Number: 2001117256
ISBN: 1-879998-24-6

Printed in the United States of America

The 2001 reprinting of this book was made possible
by the generous contribution of

Mr. & Mrs. Stephen Walker

Other books by
Rousas John Rushdoony

The Institutes of Biblical Law, Vol. I
The Institutes of Biblical Law, Vol. II, Law & Society
The Institutes of Biblical Law, Vol. III, The Intent of the Law
Systematic Theology (2 volumes)
Hebrews, James & Jude
The Gospel of John
Romans & Galatians
Thy Kingdom Come
Foundations of Social Order
The "Atheism" of the Early Church
The Biblical Philosophy of History
The Messianic Character of American Education
The Philosophy of the Christian Curriculum
Christianity and the State
Salvation and Godly Rule
God's Plan for Victory
Politics of Guilt and Pity
Roots of Reconstruction
The One and the Many
Revolt Against Maturity
By What Standard?
Law & Liberty

For a complete listing of available books
by Rousas John Rushdoony and other
Christian reconstructionists, contact:

ROSS HOUSE BOOKS
PO Box 67
Vallecito, CA 95251
www.rosshousebooks.org

Contents

Foreword

By Mark Rousas Rushdoony

The republication of this work by my father is personally very gratifying. This was the first of his writings that I studied carefully. It was used as a text for an American History class I took as a senior at Fairfax Christian School in Fairfax, Virginia some thirty years ago. Lectures and quizzes were based on the text in which we were given prior reading assignments and encouraged to underline as we read. I used it soon afterward for college writing assignments, including one on the legal issues of the War of Independence, and later for teaching in Christian schools. I still use that personal copy. By repetitive use, it has come to have a lasting effect on my thinking.

But most importantly, this series of essays gives important insight into American history by one who was more than an expert on the facts of America's history. His extensive reading (for over half a century he averaged well over a book a day) led him to an understanding of the ideas and individuals that have influenced history. Looking backward at American history, he could trace American development in terms of the ideas which gave it direction. At the heart of these ideas he saw man's faith as determinative of the direction of his history. Culture, he would later say, is religion externalized. The author never dwelt on the factual trivia of history (though he came to have an amazing and almost encyclopedic knowledge of many subjects), but on the faith-based ideas behind its various movements. Individually and collectively, men act in terms of what they believe. History, like culture, is the outworking of what men and nations have believed. Therefore, what we believe makes a difference. What we believe about our nature, truth, the source of divinity and authority, our position in the cosmos, and ethics makes a profound impact on our thought and activity. The author of these essays was at his best in tracing the ideas which became flesh and blood (and all too often enslaved humanity and shed blood) in history.

In looking forward, however, we also determine our course by what we believe. This includes what we believe about our past. If Satan is the father of lies, then it behooves Christians to sort out the truth from the abundance of lies that too often control our thinking and us. To the extent that our thoughts and actions are governed by lies, we give ourselves over to service in the kingdom of man rather than that of God. After reading these essays, it will be apparent to the reader that the author would have no part in the modern notion that the United States was founded by secular deists. On the contrary, he saw an early America that was deeply steeped in a presumption of the truth of Biblical faith and a Calvinistic perspective. The extent to which our founding fathers were, in fact, reflecting other non-Christian thinking is exceeded many times over by most of their modern critics.

Much has changed since these essays were written in 1962. Most notably, the reserve of Christian capital in the minds and morals of Americans and the institutions of our nation has been largely spent. On the other hand, there are today perhaps more Christians who are willing to take action to reverse this trend, at least within the spheres of their familial and vocational authority. This was the focus of most of my father's work. He saw the great change in America as being one of a loss of Christian faith that was working its influence throughout the culture, replaced increasingly by an anti-Christian, humanistic faith. Thus, unlike many conservatives of the early 1960's, he did not see political action as a means of restoration. That, he believed, would only come from an increase in Christian faith and commitment and its outworking in society.

These essays will greatly alter your understanding of, and appreciation for, American history. The discussions of the legal relationship between the crown and colonies, prominent in legislative appeals of the time, is now rarely mentioned. The idea of sovereignty is addressed as a theological tenet foreign to colonial political thought and the Constitution. The importance of land is noted as a consequence of the belief in "inheriting the land" as a future blessing, not an immediate economic asset.

Scattered about these pages are little bombshells that will change how you understand much of American history: that federalism owed its familiar roots to the localism of feudalism, how property and its local control is a guarantee of liberty, that federal elections were long considered of less importance than local politics, that early American ideas attributed to democratic thought were based on religious ideals of communion and community, or how ludicrous is the modern notion of a mathematical concept of equality when applied to people.

These essays do not represent mere flag-waving, however. They contain some controversial stands. The author chastises the north for its centralizing of authority to the detriment of liberty and the Constitution, yet rejects the South's irresponsible counter-position of state sovereignty. He condemns both integration and segregation (this in 1962) as "interferences with freedom of association."[1] He strongly denounces statism, but is no friend of total democracy, and called John Locke, something of a conservative hero, a majoritarian philosopher of the Glorious Revolution which allowed for parliamentary absolutism.

The author of these essays was never shy about taking a moral stand. He sought to make his outlook avowedly Christian and Scriptural. To him, the Christian faith was about submitting life and thought to righteousness as revealed in God's Word. These essays are a small portion of his attempt to do that.

Mark Rousas Rushdoony
May 9, 2001

---

[1] The author's use of the term "Negro" should be understood in terms of its appropriateness in 1962. Its use has subsequently, of course, been dropped in favor of other terms, and these may soon prove to be dated as well. My father was willing to offend with truth, but not with ungraciousness. My father was no friend of racism, having suffered some hurtful discriminatory treatment for his Armenian ethnicity early in life. Less than a year before he died, I asked him for his feelings on the Confederate battle flag on the state flags of three Southern states, then the subject of attempts at removal. His reply was, "If I were black I would find it offensive."

"… As, under the present operation of the Boston Port Bill, thousands of our respected brethren in that town must necessarily be reduced to great distress, they feel themselves affected with the sincerest sympathy and most cordial commisseration; and as they expect, under GOD, that the final deliverance of America will be owing, in a great degree, to a continuance of their virtuous struggle, they esteem themselves bound in duty and interest, to afford them every assistance and alleviation in their power.

"May this notification, by some faithful record, be handed down to the yet unborn descendants of Americans, that nothing but the most fatal necessity could have wrested the present inestimable enjoyments from their ancestors. Let them universally inculcate upon their beloved offspring an investigation of those truths, respecting both civil and religious liberty, which have been so clearly and fully stated in this generation. May they be carefully taught in all their schools, and may they never rest, until, through a Divine blessing upon their efforts, true freedom and liberty shall reign triumphant over the whole Globe…."

Recommendation of Townships of Monmouth County,
New Jersey, 1774.

"And now, my fellow-citizens of this independent republic, my fellow-Christians of every order and denomination in this assembly, and all you that fear God and hear me this day, give audience.

"The Most High planted our fathers, a small handful, in this Jeshimon, and lo! we, their posterity, have arisen up to three millions of people. (Deut. 10:22). Our ears have heard, and our fathers have told us, the marvellous things God did for them; but our eyes have seen far more glorious things done for us, whereof we are glad and rejoice this day."

Rev. Ezra Stiles, President of Yale College,
May 8th, 1783, Election Sermon,
Hartford, Connecticut.

"Now, to bring about government by oligarchy masquerading as democracy, it is fundamentally essential that practically all authority and control be centralized in our National Government."

Franklin Delano Roosevelt
March 2, 1930.

Introduction

"It is indeed high time that we repossess the important historical truth that religion was a fundamental cause of the American Revolution."[1] It is, moreover, high time that we recognize the religious presuppositions undergirding many non-religious aspects of colonial history. Towards this end, these studies have been made. They were first presented as a series of lectures to an Intercollegiate Society of Individualists' Conference held at St. Mary's College, August 20-31, 1962.

The studies best explain themselves. It should perhaps be noted that some time has been given, as the first chapter evidences, to counteracting what Boorstin, in an essay of that title, has called "The Myth of an American Enlightenment."[2]

The roots of American history go deep. Not only is it the oldest of Western countries in consecutive and unbroken inheritance in civil government, having been free of revolutions and internal chaos, but its origins are Christian and Augustinian, deeply rooted in Reformation, medieval, and patristic history. It is held, moreover, that the United States, from its origins in the Colonial period on through the era of the Constitution, represented a *Protestant feudal restoration*. This, then, is the perspective of this work.

[1.] Carl Bridenbaugh, *Mitre and Sceptre: Transcendental Faith, Ideas, Personalities, and Politics, 1689-1775* (New York: Oxford University Press, 1962), xiv.
[2.] Daniel J. Boorstin, *America and the Image of Europe* (New York: Meridian, 1960), 65-78.

When reference is made to the Christian nature of the United States, the objection immediately raised is the *absence* of reference to Christianity in the Constitution. The Constitution would never have been ratified had such reference been made, and to safeguard themselves, the people sought and gained the further protection of the First Amendment. Its wording is significant: "*Congress* shall make no laws respecting an establishment of religion, or prohibiting the free exercise thereof." All the constituent states had in some form or other either a Christian establishment or settlement, or specifically Christian legislation. Religious tests for citizenship, blasphemy laws, singular or plural establishments, and other religious settlements were the rule, jealously guarded and prized, first against British interference, then against Federal usurpation. To preserve the integrity and freedom of the specific forms of Christian statehood of the constituent states, the Constitution forbade any jurisdiction to the Federal Union in this area. The answer to the present federal interference, wrongly based on the Fourteenth Amendment, is not a Christian Amendment but the restoration of the prior jurisdiction of the states.

The American Revolution was not a revolution in the modern sense of that word. Moreover, it was a defensive war, fought to preserve American liberties from the usurpation and invasion of Parliament. The colonies rightly charged the crown with breach of feudal contract, whereby they could declare that contract null and void. The Constitution was not designed to make the United States a "nation," but to federate already existing states, whose previous unity had been primarily in the British monarch and was now in the Federal Union. As a result, the term "United States" was a plural noun, taking a plural verb. The constituent states being various forms of Christian states, they forbade the Federal Government to enter the area of religion to impose *or* forbid any establishment or settlement alien to the states. The freedom contemplated, therefore, was not freedom of or from religion, but *for* religion in the constituent states.

The states thus were prior and determinative in this and other areas. But, more important, in most of the key areas, the *counties* were the basic and determinative unit of American civil government. Not only did many local religious laws prevail with the central force of public support and legal power, but also the two other great arms of civil power were in the hands of the county: first, the power to tax property, and, second, criminal law. This is the heart and genius of the American civil structure, and the center of its resistance to tyranny. Hence the assault of federal, state, and metropolitan government planners on the county unit. Hence the proposal, as currently in California, to do away with county assessors and to remove control of property from the county unit.[3] The revival and

3. "State Ponders Tax Structure Axe for County Assessors?," *Los Angeles Herald-Examiner*, 4 October 1963, A-20.

growth of the historic American settlement depends therefore on the Christian renewal of the citizenry and the renewal of the centrality of the local units of government. Not in Washington, but on the local level, the battle will be won or lost. The key resistance today is therefore to be found among those who battle for the integrity and independence from usurpation of the county government, among those who establish and further Christian schools, among those, in short, who realize that the American answer to the problem of civil power was originally a Christian one, and firmly anchored close to home.

1

Language and Liberty

History is in part not only a long struggle for the minds, bodies, and properties of men, with various movements seeking control of historical processes in terms of their faith, but it is also a battle with respect to language. An instrument of power at Babel, language was, according to Scripture, confused by God in order to create diversity and the possibility of separate and integral developments. Men fail to understand one another not only when they speak alien tongues, but also when they use the same words with very diverse meanings. Communists and conservative U. S. Republicans alike use the word "republic," but with radically different interpretations. Christians and relativists both speak of "law" with no identity of meaning. Again, the definition of "liberty" is not limited to its nine dictionary definitions but has, in its civil and religious connotations, almost as many meanings as there are political parties and religions in existence. As a result, the very fact of a common tongue and an identical word can sometimes, on the presupposition of a necessary cultural unity, further the confusion of speech. As a result, many cults and movements have sought at times a private and esoteric speech only to find staleness and flatness of definition from lack of public conflict.

Moreover, in general usage, words and communication-forms change, and they sometimes change so slowly that the erosion is imperceptible even when complete. The world of art gives many startling illustrations of this process. Thus, one of the central triumphs of the Christian faith, often celebrated in Christian art, was the ascension of Christ. This glorious victory was gradually altered, without any radical changes at any one time,

1

to emphasize not only the human form of Christ, but also the pictorial qualities currently of interest. The ascension formula became the vehicle also of pictures of the assumption of the Virgin Mary, and then, as Mary became more and more an attractive woman rather than a religious principle, the picture became openly an avowed glorification of Venus. A telling instance of this change is found in the work of Peter Paul Rubens (1577-1640), as witness his *Apotheosis of the Duke of Buckingham* and *The Apotheosis of James I*. Rubens seemed unaware of the blasphemy involved in his paintings. Again, in Rubens' *Nature Adorned by the Graces*, there is a total absence of the Franciscan view of nature as God's creation; rather, we see the many-breasted Diana of the Ephesians. Every trace of a Christian conception of nature is missing. Rubens thus moved in a world where Christ ruled in the church and pagan nature governed the world. A confusion in language and communication reflects usually a cultural confusion, but not necessarily a personal confusion. Many a man uses a language implying an alien faith without an awareness of the divergence of meaning.

A major instance of this is the usage of such terms as reason, natural law, social contract or compact, and related ones in the seventeenth and especially eighteenth centuries. A contemporary historian has remarked on the coincidence of language and divergence of meanings among various parties in France before and during the Revolution. This was no less true of colonial America. The refusal to recognize this divergence of meaning is behind the common ascription of Deism to many eighteenth century Americans. Actually, Deism was a late arrival in America, and very slight in extent and influence prior to the American Revolution.[1]

The language of Reason and Nature had a long philosophical and legal history and was by no means the property of any one school. In 1632, the royal charter to Maryland stipulated that the laws of its legislative body must be "consonant to reason." In 1644, the Presbyterian, Samuel Rutherford, in *Lex Rex*, cited Aristotle and Aquinas and appealed to "God and nature." In 1645, *The Ancient Bounds*, an independent statement of the case for liberty of conscience, declared: "For this is a rule: The law of nature supersedes institutions. Men have a natural being before they come to have a spiritual being; they are men before they are Christians. Now therefore for faultiness in Christianity, you must not destroy the man." In 1647, Richard Overton, in *An Appeal from the Commons to the Free People*, based his argument on "reason." In 1649, *The True Levellers' Standard Advanced* spoke of "the great Creator, Reason." A common language was appealed to,

---

[1.] See Melba Paxton Wilson, *Pre-Revolutionary Liberalism and Post-Revolutionary Unitarianism in America*, unpublished study (New York: Columbia University Library, 1930). See Rev. Thomas Belsham's letter of 1809 concerning the continuing conservatism of that day, 8; and Wilson's "Conclusion," 144-149.

but with widely divergent meanings. When the pressure of this divergence of meanings brought about a collapse into meaninglessness of the words, then new words, such as "democracy," began to supplant the eroded terms.

As has been noted, many men use words which to others imply a religious view not held by the speaker or writer without an awareness either of the divergence of meaning or the mixed presuppositions. Witness, for example, Rev. John Witherspoon (1722-1794), a Presbyterian leader who in 1768 assumed the presidency of the College of New Jersey (now Princeton University). Witherspoon taught many who later played an active role in American life. His own belief in sound money, mixed government, and a division of powers was pronounced. An orthodox Calvinist, Witherspoon, without any sense of contradiction, also followed the philosophy of Thomas Reid (1710-1796), Scottish realism, using this questionable tool against Hume, Deism, and French philosophers. In his *Lectures on Moral Philosophy*, he spoke the language of rights and reason, combining with this man-centered emphasis his own theocentric faith. Witherspoon's students, profoundly influenced by him, reached positions of eminence in the Constitutional Convention and in early United States history. They included a president, vice-president, ten cabinet officers, twenty-one senators, thirty-nine congressmen, and twelve governors, as well as other public figures. All these were affected by Witherspoon's Calvinism, classicism, and Common-Sense philosophy. This confusion, however, was slight in contrast to other phenomena of the American scene. Thus, in 1642, in Maryland, a group of "Protestant Catholics" filed complaints against Thomas Gerard, lord of St. Clement's Manor and an influential Roman Catholic planter, for depriving them of their books and the key to their chapel. About a century later, Pennsylvania saw a Protestant, Conrad Beissel, a religious hermit, establish his Ephrata Colony, the Coalico cloisters, with men and women submitting to sacerdotal celibacy and asceticism.

The Puritans of New England and colonials elsewhere combined a horror of Rome with a dedication to Scholasticism, as James J. Walsh has shown in the *Education of the Founding Fathers of the Republic* (1935), a study of Scholasticism at Harvard, William and Mary, Yale, Princeton, Pennsylvania, Columbia, and Brown.[2] The reliance of the Puritans on the logic of the Aristotelian, Peter Ramus (d. 1572), has been well documented by Perry Miller in *The New England Mind: The Seventeenth Century*. John Cotton (1585-1652), Puritan divine, whose able *Exposition of First John* has been reprinted as late as 1962, noted the extensive influence of the "Schoolmen." Scholasticism in philosophy, which gave much authority to

---

[2.] See also Richard M. Gummere, "Some Classical Sidelights on Colonial Education," *The Classical Journal*, 55, no. 5 (February 1960), 223-232.

man's unaided reason, was increasingly combined with Puritanism in theology.

Furthermore, natural law had, as C. H. McIlwaine, in *The American Revolution: A Constitutional Interpretation*, points out, a legal status, in that it was held to be "engrafted into the British constitution," so that appeal to it was not only philosophical and theological, but also juridical. The language of the day was thus not the property of Deism but of all parties.

But were not Benjamin Franklin and Thomas Jefferson very obviously Deists? That both were familiar with Deism goes without saying; Franklin also greatly admired the evangelist Whitefield, and yet was on the fringes, at the very least, of the infamous Hell Fire Club in England. He was also a member of the Neuf Soeurs, which held a commemorative assembly on his death.[3] Jedidiah Morse charged Jefferson with being an Illuminatus; while Jefferson denied this charge, he still defended Weishaupt as "an enthusiastic philanthropist."[4] Federalism was, as Merle Curti pointed out in *The Growth of American Thought* (1943), the American reaction against the Enlightenment. The Jeffersonian Republicans represented a party favorable to France, and yet were in actuality closer to the Federalists, at times furthering policies inimical to Jacobin theory, than they were to the Enlightenment and to France. The differences between Republicans and the European Enlightenment were far greater and more basic than the differences between Federalists and Republicans. The issues between these two parties became increasingly more and more sectional and local rather than philosophical. Jefferson spoke with no small measure of truth when he observed, "We are all republicans—we are all federalists." The eclectic approach of both Franklin and Jefferson to all things made them ready samplers of any thought. But were they Deists? Vergilius Ferm has defined Deism as, first, the view that "God has no immediate relation with the world...the 'absentee landlord' view," and, second, that "revelation is superfluous, that reason is touchstone to religious validity, that religion and ethics are natural phenomena, that the traditional God need hardly be appealed to since man finds in nature the necessary guides for moral and religious living."[5] In terms of this, let us examine the plea for public prayer given by Benjamin Franklin on June 28, 1787, at the Constitutional Convention:

> In this situation of this assembly, groping as it were in the dark to find the political truth, and scarce able to distinguish it when presented to us, how has it happened, sir, that we have not hitherto once thought

3. Una Birch, *Secret Societies and the French Revolution* (London: John Lane, 1911), 31-33. For Franklin and Dashwood's group, see Daniel P. Mannix, *The Hell Fire Club* (New York: Ballantine, 1959).

4. Nesta H. Webster, *World Revolution* (London: Constable, 1921), 79.

5. Ferm in Dagobert D. Runes, *Dictionary of Philosophy*, fifteenth edition, revised (New York: Philosophical Library, 1960), 75.

of humbly applying to the Father of Lights to illuminate our understandings? In the beginning of the contest with Great Britain, when we were sensible to danger, we had daily prayers in this room for divine protection.

Our prayers, sir, were heard, and they were graciously answered. All of us who were engaged in the struggle must have observed frequent instances of a superintending Providence in our favor. To that kind Providence we owe this happy opportunity of consulting in peace on the means of establishing our future national felicity. And have we now forgotten that powerful friend? Or do we imagine that we no longer need His assistance? I have lived, sir, a long time, and the longer I live, the more convincing proofs I see of this truth—that God governs the affairs of men.

And if a sparrow cannot fall to the ground without His notice, is it probable an empire can rise without His aid? We have been assured, sir, in the sacred writings, that except the Lord build the house, they labor in vain that build it.

I firmly believe this; and I also believe that without this concurring aid we shall succeed in this political building no better than the builders of Babel; we shall be divided by our partial little local interests; our projects will be confounded and we ourselves shall become a byword down the future ages. And what is worse, mankind may hereafter, from this unfortunate instance, despair of establishing governments by human wisdom and leave it to chance, war and conquest.[6]

Consider also these earnest words of Thomas Jefferson:

Can the liberties of a nation be sure when we remove their only firm basis, a conviction in the minds of the people, that these liberties are the gift of God? that they are not to be violated but with His wrath? Indeed, I tremble for my country, when I reflect that God is just; that His justice cannot sleep forever; that a revolution of the wheel of fortune, a change of situation, is among possible events; that it may become probable by supernatural interference! The Almighty has no attribute which can take side with us in that event.

That both these men were influenced by Deism, among other things, is certainly to be granted, but, unless one writes these statements off as the most arrant kind of hypocrisy, it becomes equally clear that even stronger colonial influences were at work. Here, in clear and forthright language from these men, is Calvinism's predestination and total providence, and, at the same time, the near Unitarian exclusion of Christ from the Godhead. God is not seen as an absentee landlord, and not merely reason but more than reason is appealed to. It becomes clear that, in view of the mixed linguistic, religious, and philosophical premises, *no facile classification can be*

---

6. The Convention did not accede to Franklin's plea, fearing that the introduction of a chaplain would lead the public to believe that the Convention was disunited.

ventured. To call Jefferson and Franklin Deists[7] is as erroneous as to call Jonathan Edwards either a Calvinist or a latter-day champion of New England orthodoxy. Edwards was strongly influenced by Platonism, disregarded the basic New England faith in a holy commonwealth, was a thorough empiricist, and sought to ground Christian faith on Locke and Newton. In terms of this, he could affirm that

> ... it is self-evident I believe to every man, that Space is necessary, eternal, infinite and omnipresent. But I had as good speak plain: I have already said as much as, that Space is God. And it is indeed clear to me, that all the Space there is, not proper to body, all the Space there is without the bounds of Creation, all the Space there was before the Creation, is God himself; and no body would in the least pick at it, if it were not because of the gross conceptions, that we have of Space.[8]

Many of Edwards' ostensibly "liberal" critics were, in terms of New England orthodoxy, more conservative than he. Edwards' emphasis on experimental religion was the analogue to the Arminian emphasis on works and the empirical demand for phenomena. Theologically, some of the implications of Edwards' position are more radical than anything in Franklin, while other elements are intensely conservative. *Classification can thus be falsification.*

However, our current classifications are not to be despised. They are the product of a development, refinement, distillation, and self-analysis of thought and are excellent scholarly tools. Without them, historical research would become meaningless. But it must not be forgotten that Colonial America must also be understood in terms of the meaning and purpose of man and society in their day, in terms of their *faith, inheritance,* and *goal.* The linguistic confusion, and the philosophical confusion, must be noted, as well as the "bandwagon" use of language, the association of varying ideas around a concept which has gained currency.

As we shall see, the social contract, which meant to continental philosophers and Deists a *statist* concept, a contract between people and state, meant, as did the laws of nature and of reason, a strongly *anti-statist* concept to the Americans. For them it represented their feudal-born concept of local and federal government, limited in nature. Although they often assumed that continental thinkers meant what Americans did, they nonetheless held to a very different concept and developed their civil polity into channels markedly in contrast to the French Revolution. A language which elsewhere pointed to statism, in America was the vehicle of native

---

[7.] For a recent attempt to analyze Washington's religious faith as liberal, see Paul F. Boller Jr., *George Washington and Religion* (Dallas, Texas: Southern Methodist University Press, 1963).

[8.] Jonathan Edwards, "Notes on Natural Science of Being," in Carl Van Doren, ed., *Benjamin Franklin and Jonathan Edwards, Selections from their Writings* (New York: Scribner, 1920), 223.

conceptions of liberty. The studied rootlessness, based on scientific and rationalistic premises, which the French Revolution sought was anathema to Jefferson, a friend of the French, and on such grounds Jefferson saw little hope for independence movements in South America: "They will fall under military despotism, and become the murderous tools of their respective Bonapartes." Both the closeness and distance of Jefferson to French thought can be cited; the major factor was a differing tradition, and Jefferson's roots in that American tradition. Jefferson cannot be understood apart from an understanding of these particular roots. Men speak not only in a verbal language but also in the language of history, in the context and meaning of their time and place. It was the language of American colonial history which was written into the Constitution of the United States. With reference to the European and classical sources so often cited by the shapers of American history, "not only Locke and Montesquieu, but Aristotle and Cicero and Plutarch, Hobbes, Burlamaqui, Milton, Hooker, Bolingbroke, Blackstone, Burke, Shaftesbury and a score of collateral branches," Burnham's comment is apropos:

> But the Fathers were the masters, not the victims, of these inherited ideas, and sometimes it is the rhetoric more than the ideas that is taken over. The Fathers were protected from ideology not only by piety and a native skepticism toward abstract reason, but by their persistent sense of fact, of the specific.[9]

In spite of this pragmatic usage, there was, however, an element of philosophical indistinction which must be recognized. The epistemological self-consciousness granted by two centuries of development cannot be read backwards into history, but neither can modern secularism be so read into it. To speak, therefore, of an "American Enlightenment"[10] is to attempt to read into the Revolution a later development in American thought. Again, to seek there the developed Christian orthodoxy of today is also to misread history.

---

[9]. James Burnham, *Congress and the American Tradition* (Chicago: Regnery, 1959), 24.
[10]. Russel Blaine Nye, *The Cultural Life of the New Nation, 1776-1830* (New York: Harper and Row, 1960).

2

Feudalism and Federalism

The difficulty in discussing feudalism rests not only in its complex structure, but also in its long history which embraces conditions both good and bad. The evils of feudalism were real enough, but its virtues were equally notable. Lynn White Jr. has noted that "Evidence is accumulating to show that a serf in the turbulent and insecure tenth century enjoyed a standard of living considerably higher than that of a proletarian in the reign of Augustus."[1]

The term "feudalism" is itself relatively modern and covers one major aspect of life in the "feudal era." One of the most notable aspects of that period is that its structure was by no means exclusively feudal. The total structure was the product of a variety of causes. The breakdown of central authority, and the growth of political anarchy and personal insecurity, led to a necessity for local power and protection. Added to this was the economic collapse, the breakdown of state-controlled economies. As a result, many indigenous elements developed or asserted themselves. As Fustel de Coulanges has pointed out, *The Ancient City* was a religious and political unit, a bond of heaven and earth, as the Greek *polis* had been. Villages, Teutonic and otherwise, asserted this religious independence. Alods, lands held in full ownership without any feudal ties, were an important factor in the situation. The local military power sought to establish its power over landholders and villages and create a network of federated powers.

---

1. "Technology and Invention in the Middle Ages," *Speculum*, 15 (1940), 151.

Moreover, as central statist law declined in its effectiveness, contract increasingly became a basis for both personal and civil law.[2] The social contract theory of the eighteenth century was a philosophical reworking of an aspect of European history which actually destroyed whatever validity the contractual aspect of society had by total reference to state sovereignty rather than to local practices and self-government. Contract had been non-statist government in the main, but was reworked into a justification of the sovereign state.

Most basic to the feudal structure was Christianity. Ironically, major studies of feudal law, politics, and society have been written without any reference to this fact. Christianity, with its faith in the transcendental God as the source of authority, challenged and defeated the ancient city-state concept, in which absolute power was immanent, sundered the mystical bond of heaven and earth, denied the divinity of the state (whether of office or persons, i.e., of the rulers, or of people), and challenged the centralized and immanent unity of life after the pattern of the Tower of Babel. The basic pagan principle of a necessary human unity in the forms of state power, in which ultimate authority was immanently realized, was denied in favor of a transcendental unity. Religion had previously existed as social cement, a necessary aspect of statist life. Now the church had entered the picture to shatter the pagan and Babel-like unity. As against the universal incarnation of God and man in the state, with divinity and humanity commingled and confused, Christianity asserted the unique incarnation, without confusion, of God and man in Jesus Christ. No other unity of the two orders was possible. *The state was thus placed under God, not in the being of God as in paganism.* The state, in terms of the Council of Chalcedon, could not be regarded as the order of man's fulfilment nor of his redemption. Rome fell in 410, and the Council of Chalcedon met in 451. The two events are not unrelated. What the barbarians did to the City of Rome, the Council did to the idea of Rome, and of all states and empires. Wherever, as in the East, there was a revival of Roman and pagan theory, there was a necessary war against the implications of Chalcedon.[3] In the West, the pagan conception of kingship and state was widely present and often successfully asserted, but always with reviving resistance from Christianity. The feudal order was not without its areas of paganism, but European feudalism is to be sharply distinguished from all other ostensible feudalisms at this point: while sometimes at war with the church, it was still

---

2. For contract and feudalism, see Sidney Painter, *Feudalism and Liberty* (Baltimore: Johns Hopkins Press, 1961), 245ff.
3. See Gerhard B. Ladner, "Origin and Significance of the Byzantine Iconoclastic Controversy," *Medieval Studies*, 11, (1940), 127-149. Published for the Pontifical Institute of Medieval Studies by Sheed and Ward, New York. For a brief study of the Christian origin of the limited state, see Gerhart Niemeyer, "Two Socialisms," *Modern Age*, vol. 6, no. 4 (Fall 1962), 367-377.

governed in part by Christian faith and the Christian ascription of true sovereignty to God alone.

Again, under paganism each religio-political entity or order had one total law. Under feudalism, a variety of laws governing various areas became the order of the day and were pushed to the limits. There was village law, fief law (and common law in England was in part law common to England as one great fief under Norman kings), church or canon law, Roman law, merchant law, Jewish law, and so on. Law was thus class and sphere law, and sometimes contract law. A great variety of courts and jurisdictions existed, each strictly limited in its sway. The modern conception of state law, total in its scope and jurisdiction, was thus alien to feudalism.

Law was also basically *local*. Some appeal existed, as witness the *commendation*, whereby, upon certain offenses by the lord, such as "counsel against his (the vassal's) life," which meant failure to provide protection. Or, "if the lord has committed adultery with the wife of the vassal," Louis the Pious, to cite an instance, in 816 decreed the dissolution of the feudal relationship.

Moreover, the system of *immunity* increased the local power as against the central in the Frankish Empire. The privileges granted by immunity were transfers to local government of what had been prerogatives of central power. First, freedom from taxation, or the privilege of local collection by the proprietor rather than an officer of the monarch, was granted. Second, immunity surrendered various sources of state income to the new proprietor. Third, the count, the king's officer, was excluded from the territory covered by immunity except for social functions and in cases involving denial of justice or abuse of power.

Furthermore, the basic structure of society was *the local land unit*. *Property and power* were thus very closely linked, whereas in contemporary society they have been increasingly separated.

Feudalism was to a degree a Christian society, based on the Biblical concept of the limitation and division of all powers and the denial of divinity to the human order. It was, of course, by no means free of paganism and sought constantly to enmesh the church into its systems of feudal ties and contracts and thus negate the freedom of the church. By means of claims over church lands, and marriages with the secular clergy, this was extensively furthered, and bishops became the vassals and creatures of lords and kings. The church, to extricate itself, imposed celibacy on the secular clergy in order to break the feudal control of the church. Feudalism thus was at war with the church, and also with the growing power of the state, with its claim to absolutism, a denial of all the legal limitations imposed on the monarch by feudalism. The feudal order was, with all its pagan elements, more than a product of social circumstances: it was also a form of Christian order. The failure of scholars to note this constitutes a serious omission.[4]

The social contract theory, as has been noted, was in part a modern reinterpretation of an aspect of earlier Western life. It presupposed early feudal and pre-feudal Europe as the state of nature, assuming a cultural condition to be the natural fact. Moreover, with many, the state of nature tended to become, not the arena of disorder, but the assured world of the Franciscan state of nature. The Franciscan faith viewed nature, not as demonic, but as a fellow creature of God, an area to be viewed with confidence: "brother sun," "sister moon," "brother fire," and even "sister death." Time also became an area of fulfilment together with the world, and Roger Bacon (1214-1294), a Franciscan friar, stated the premises for the scientific conquest of creation by Christian man.[5] This perspective had its culmination in Calvinism; the Christian saw nature with expectancy: while it was to be destroyed and recreated, yet it was also the area of fulfilment. It was, like man, fallen, and hence not normative, but, like man and time, to be redeemed. In decided contrast, in the developed view of the Enlightenment, nature was good and the state of nature both primary and normative. The true function of the state, by means of the scientific dictatorship of the elite, was to restore the state of nature, true anarchy.

As the power of the expanding states grew and statism began to assert its claims, the argument of its enemies was in terms of the feudal conception of society as held together by contractual agreement. Whether in papal deposition of kings, the protection of Protestant minorities, or the claims of Commons against king, the contractual nature of authority and power was argued. This feudal, contractual conception had then its varying applications, as has been noted. "It was used by the Englishman John Locke to justify the Glorious Revolution of 1688. It was an axiom of revolutionary political opinion in eighteenth-century France, being popularized by Rousseau. It played its part in forming a revolutionary sentiment among the American colonies. The origin of the United States, therefore, goes back to feudal principles of government."[6]

The differences between these three revolutions are notable. To the extent that the social contract theory described the contract as one between people and state, rather than a complexity of contracts between people, groups, and persons, to that extent statism benefited by the doctrine, in that power was conferred upon the monarch or state.

[4.] For examples, see Edward Jenks, *Law and Politics in the Middle Ages*, (New York: Holt, 1898); and Rushton Coulborn, ed., *Feudalism in History*, (Princeton, New Jersey: Princeton University Press, 1956).
[5.] See Albert T. Mollegen, *Christianity and Modern Man* (Indianapolis: Bobbs-Merrill, 1961), 56f.
[6.] James Westfall Thompson and Edgar Nathaniel Johnson, *An Introduction to Medieval Europe, 300-1500* (New York: Norton, 1937), 305.

In England, William the Conqueror both furthered feudalism in some areas and fought against it in others. His role gained a symbolic significance, in that the tradition of English liberty and constitutionalism is in part an anti-Norman and anti-royal faith. Cromwell's soldiers, and other Englishmen as well, often viewed their work as the restoration of English liberties subverted by Norman kings. A Christian commonwealth and true English liberties were not only to be attained but also restored. The royal power had claimed sovereignty over both the people as a civil body and the people as a church. The control or seizure of church headship was long a goal of royal power. Popular sentiment was not wanting in support of this measure, but, in very great measure, other tendencies also had great popular support. First, the tradition of Lollardy continued until the Reformation as a vital factor, and one of Tyndale's first publications was a long forbidden Lollard tract. Its hostility extended to both crown and church.[7] Second, feudal localism retained its hold on the common mind. The Robin Hood stories represent in part this popularity of feudal localism as against the king's power and the king's sheriff. Third, Magna Carta, 1215, so extensively used in English legal and political tradition and in American claims against Parliament and crown, is a feudal document, a defense of a waning feudal order. "Nearly all the rights listed in the sixty-three chapters of Magna Carta relate to the feudal system which was becoming obsolete even in King John's time. Because many of its provisions sought to restore the old feudal relationships it was, to this extent, a conservative document."[8] Magna Carta granted, among other things, freedom to the Church of England, no taxation without representation of property owners, the rights of the City of London, constitution of a general council of the kingdom, trial by peers, no forcible seizure without due process of law, and liberty to leave and enter the kingdom. In sum, the king's absolutism was denied, and the king placed under feudal law. The principle of contract was strongly affirmed. Innocent III nullified Magna Carta on the ground that it had been extorted by force. It is noteworthy that in August, 1297, when the barons sought the confirmation of the charter from Edward I, they complained of the requirements of foreign military service. The U.S. Constitution entered a prohibition against involuntary or drafted foreign military service, a legal statement with a long feudal history.

The feudal order, as so often presented, established a wide variety of legal fences against man's activity. Trade, buying and selling, was in particular the subject of constant legislation as time passed, but the legislation represented in part new claims made by church and state. *Laissez faire* has

---

[7.] See Thomas Cuming Hall, *The Religious Background of American Culture* (Boston: Little Brown, 1930).

[8.] Richard L. Perry and John C. Cooper, *Sources of our Liberties* (American Bar Foundation, 1952), 9.

some roots in feudal law, in that the feudal law of merchants defined trade as a separate legal sphere. Significantly, the Peace of God, which, at the Synod of Charroux, 989, was extended to mean the immunity of churches and clergymen, later had this aspect: "No one shall seize or rob merchants." The extent of medieval regulations has been greatly exaggerated and misunderstood. The ideas of a just price and a just wage were not abstract concepts but had reference to "common estimation in or by the market." And, apart from usury, "the scholastics and canonists generally exercised great care not to lay down precepts which would interfere unnecessarily with the pursuit by individuals of legitimate economic gain."[9]

As against the complex structure of feudal society, a number of levelling forces have been at work since the late middle ages. Monarchy was instrumental in nullifying the authority of feudalism and furthering statism. Tocqueville noted the similar social effects of radical democrats and absolute monarchs: "In France the kings have always been the most active and the most constant of levellers."[10] What monarchy began, democracy continued, being in essence a similar political theory, holding also to the absolutism of the state and its masters.

The question of freedom is first of all a question of sovereignty and of responsibility. Who is sovereign, and to whom is man responsible? This source of sovereignty is also the source of freedom. If sovereignty resides in God and is only held ministerially by men, then the basic responsibility of ruler and ruled is to God, who is also the source of freedom. But if sovereignty resides in the state, whether a monarchy or democracy, man has no appeal beyond the law of the state, and no source of ethics apart from it. He is totally responsible to that order and has only those rights which the state chooses to confer upon him. The word *comprehend* means both "to contain" and "to understand." That which *contains* man is also the source of our *understanding* of man. If man is a creature of the state, then he is to be understood in terms of the state. Aristotle's man, a social animal, can never transcend his political order. Christian man, however, created in the image of God, cannot be contained in anything short of God's eternal decree and order, nor understood except in terms of God Himself. Man therefore is not understandable in terms of man but in terms of God. Absolute monarchy and democracy, statism in other words, came into existence as revivals of paganism and as anti-Christian movements, whatever their ostensible claims to the contrary may be.

The American Revolution, rightfully termed by Peter F. Drucker "the American counter-revolution," was a denial of the concept of human or

---

[9.] Jacob Viner, *The Intellectual History of Laissez Faire, The Henry Simons Lectures*, vol. 2. (Chicago: The University of Chicago Law School, 1961), 52f.
[10.] Alexis de Tocqueville, *Democracy in America*, vol. I (New York: Langley, 1841), 3.

political sovereignty and an establishment of the freedom of a *classless feudalism*, a federal system of governments. It was an *anti-statist revolution*, directed, first, against the claims to absolutism by Parliament, and, second, against a monarch who refused to be a purely feudal lord to the colonies and ruled in terms of his absolutism as exercised through Parliament, i.e., "the king in Parliament." While it is popular today to use occasional references to popular sovereignty as a means of reading democracy into the revolution and Constitution, the fact remains that both revolution and Constitution were distrustful of the people, even as they were also of every group and every structure of society and government. The Bill of Rights demanded of the federal government the same immunities against statism once demanded of kings in England; it is properly a bill of *immunities* against the state and its power. Although the Constitution limited itself to express powers only, so radical was the distrust of statism that it was felt necessary to spell out the immunities by amendment.

The cleavage between Jefferson and the continental philosophers is especially apparent at this point. The French conceptions of sovereignty and centralization distressed Jefferson, who wrote to Madison, on August 28, 1789, "There is no country where the mania for over governing has taken deeper root than in France, or been the source of greater mischief." The American scene, as Tocqueville later noted, was very different: "every village forms a sort of republic accustomed to conduct its own affairs."[11] The French Revolution made a point of wiping out every trace of feudalism and localism it possibly could; the American Revolution brought localism to a new development in the form of federalism.

From the beginning, the American colonies were radically different from England while perpetuating English tradition.

> No greater contrast could be noted in the position of men than that between the Englishman at home, in the early seventeenth century, and the Englishman who emigrated to America. Almost all the conditions that surrounded the former were reversed in the case of the latter. The pressure of central government was immediately and almost completely withdrawn. Many of the most urgent activities of government in England, such as the vagabondage, almost ceased in the colonies. The class of settled rural gentry from which most local officials were drawn in England did not exist in America. On the other hand, the wilderness, the Indians, the freedom from restraint, the religious liberty, the opportunity for economic and social rise in the New World made a set of conditions which had been quite unknown in the mother-country.[12]

11. *Ibid.*, 439.
12. Edward Potts Cheyney, *European Background of American History: 1300 - 1600* (New York: Collier Books, 1961), 183.

An unusually high percentage of the men in the colonies were university men. Although "vain and light fellows" existed in their midst, they were numerically less in proportion than in England. Again, the number of dedicated Christians was remarkably high, and arguments to the contrary are simply an evasion of reality. Statistics here are worthless. Today, church membership is high and also meaningless. It was then low because it was an act requiring maturity, responsibility, and learning.

Local government flourished in the colonies. Significantly, Robin Hood's old enemy, the sheriff, became in America not the king's man but the local government's officer. Judges were also officers in the area of their jurisdiction, and the attempt, later, on the part of England to assume the pay of the judges in Massachusetts and make them, as in England, state officers, became a major source of grievance and actual defiance. Thus, in England the county had for centuries been steadily dominated by the crown and by crown officers, and locally by the gentry. In the colonies, the gentry were missing, and town and county were locally governed.[13] This development is all the more significant against the background of a contrary development in England. James I (1603-1625) took seriously his role as head of the church and absolute monarch. Thus, in 1604, he declared: "What God hath joined, then, let no man separate. I am the husband and all the whole isle is my lawful wife. I am the head and it is my body. I am the shepherd and it is my flock." In 1610 he asserted: "The state of monarchy is the supremest thing upon the earth, for kings are not only God's lieutenants upon earth and sit upon God's throne, but even by God himself they are called gods.... As to dispute what God may do is blasphemy,.... so it is sedition in subjects to dispute what a king may do in the height of his power.... Encroach not upon the prerogative of the crown; if there falls out a question that concerns my prerogative or mystery of state, deal not with it till you consult with the king or his council, or both, for they are transcendent matters."

The king of England, originally a feudal lord, although also with a background of barbarian divine kingship, was steadily transformed into an absolute monarch. Parliament, instead of destroying this absolutism, claimed and won it for itself in 1688, and now knows no other power. As a result, the king or queen of England rules through and in Parliament only, i.e., the monarch reigns and Parliament rules, by the same *divine right*. On the eve of the American Revolution, Blackstone wrote: "If the Parliament

---

[13.] For the very marked independence of the town, see Sumner Chilton Powell, *Puritan Village, the Formation of a New England Town* (Middletown, Conn.: Wesleyan University Press, 1963), notes, 117, 140. For the "large degree of autonomy ... accorded each town" by the Massachusetts General Court, 1635, see Thomas Jefferson Wertenbaker, *The Puritan Oligarchy, The Founding of American Civilization* (New York: Grosset and Dunlap, 1947), 44f: "Localism in Religion, the Congregational way, went hand in hand with localism in government."

will positively enact a thing to be done which is unreasonable, I know of no power in the ordinary form of the Constitution that is vested with authority to control it." In 1946, the Attorney General of England, Sir Hartley Shawcross, M.P., declared: "Parliament is sovereign; it may make any laws. It could ordain that all blue-eyed babies be destroyed at birth."[14]

The colonies knew the issues better than many a modern scholar. They were not indulging in myth-making or rhetoric in demanding the rights of freeborn Englishmen. They were fully aware of the precarious nature of English liberties in the past, and their perspective was not past-bound. But they did know that the original relationship between freeborn Englishmen and king was a *feudal and contractual one*. Their charge was that the king had ceased to be such a king. Again, Parliament had originally been a non-statist feudal body, a court of contract and law between king and vassals, and representation was based on feudal classes. Parliament, however, had become a statist body, exercising divine right, and George III, as a modern monarch, stood solidly behind Parliament and refused to exercise the right to veto (used by no English monarch since the beginning of the eighteenth century).

The American colonial development was a radical antithesis to the English development, the first anti-statist, the second, statist. When England began, with the French and Indian War and other international crises, to exercise its claims over the colonies, conflict, already present, became sharp and irreconcilable. Not Samuel Adams but two mutually contradictory theories of society and government brought on the American Revolution, which rested on a long, separate, and independent development.

The colonies, in resorting to feudal law, by no means turned their eyes towards the past. John Adams, in *On the Canon and the Feudal Law*, treated the medieval church and feudalism as the two greatest evils of history and accused Britain of trying to force America into past bondage, into medieval tyranny. Nonetheless, he turned to English feudal documents to justify his conception of the liberty of the free Englishmen.[15]

In terms of this feudal claim, the Declaration of Independence does not mention Parliament directly; it is a declaration of independence from the king of England, and is in terms of his violation of contract.[16] The colonial legislatures were the American parliaments, like the English parliament under a king, and no other parliament had any jurisdiction over them. The Stamp Act, 1765, had as its purpose colonial defense, a necessary item, but the colonies denied the right of Parliament to tax them on their own behalf.

[14.] Clarence Manion, *The Key to Peace* (Chicago: Heritage Foundation, 1951), 91.

[15.] John Adams, *Works*, vol. III (Boston: Little Brown, 1865), 447-464.

[16.] See Carl L. Becker, *The Declaration of Independence, a Study in the History of Political Ideas* (New York: Vintage Books, 1958).

The constitutional conflict between colonies and Parliament was brought into focus. The colonies denied, from 1765 to 1776, Parliament's authority to tax them externally or internally, while affirming their willingness to accept parliamentary legislation "for the supervision of the empire as a whole."[17] Each colony was a *free English state* under the king, and their relationship to him was feudal and contractual. This refusal of the colonies to admit outside power hindered united colonial action and hampered the Revolution.

The Declaration of Independence was thus a *constitutional* document, an assertion that a fundamental contract which had governed the colonies had been broken by the king. Massachusetts in 1773 made clear the feudal basis of its constitutional protest against British encroachments.

McIlwaine has documented the reality of the colonial claim. The legal relationship of subjects to the king remained feudal, not national. The development of theory with reference to king and Parliament in England did not nullify the king's feudal relationship to Scotland and other areas. The Whig doctrine of parliamentary sovereignty was not the American doctrine of government. "The Whigs brought on the English Revolution, but the American doctrine of 1774 was really a new revolt against one of the main principles of 1688."[18]

Some of the liberties attained by the Glorious Revolution of 1688 were prized by the colonials, but its central fact, the parliamentary claim to exercise royal absolutism, its statism, the American Revolution denied and revolted against. John Locke was the philosopher of the Glorious Revolution, and his fundamental thesis was majoritarianism.[19] To see Locke as the philosopher of the American Revolution is to misread history. Where Locke defended liberty and property, he was widely quoted; where he championed majoritarianism, he was bypassed. *The Americans, at every point, culled passages from widely divergent authorities to buttress each particular position without any departure from their own.*

With respect to the concept of limited government, *The Federalist* is instructive. Hamilton, of course, noted the fact that feudalism is a kind of federalism in no. 17. The Constitution itself he called "a limited Constitution" (no. 78), and, in discussing express powers, he saw the entire

---

17. See Edmund S. and Helen M. Morgan, *The Stamp Act Crisis: Prologue to Revolution* (Chapel Hill: Published for the Institute of Early American History and Culture at Williamsburg, Va., by the University of North Carolina Press, 1953). For British measures prior to the Stamp Act which contributed to the colonial constitutional crises, see Bernard Knollenberg, *Origin of the American Revolution: 1759-1766*, revised edition, (New York: Collier, 1961).
18. Charles Howard McIlwaine, *The American Revolution: A Constitutional Interpretation* (Ithaca, New York: Great Seat Books, Cornell, 1958), 160.
19. See Willmoore Kendall, *John Locke and the Doctrine of Majority Rule* (Urbana: University of Illinois Press, 1959). For recent developments of this in English history, see Diana Spearman, *Democracy in England* (New York: Macmillan, 1957).

Constitution as a limitation upon the federal government imposed by the people and constituent groups (no. 84). More than that, *The Federalist*, as Dietze has noted, saw federalism itself as "a form of constitutionalism.[20]

A double aspect thus characterized the new government: (1) A legal, written constitutionalism was adopted, anti-statist in nature, which affirmed the immunities of people, local governments, and colonies as against the federal government, thereby underscoring the purpose of the Revolution. (2) The Federal structure of the United States, beginning with free, self-government and responsible men, townships, counties, and then states and the federal union, itself constituted a constitution, so that *written and structural constitutions* confirmed and reinforced one another.

This union was seen as pluralistic, not national. Again, references to nationalism are to be found, but the essential usage was to the contrary. As Bryce noted much later:

> A few years ago the American Protestant Episcopal Church was occupied at its triennial Convention in revising its liturgy. It was thought desirable to introduce among the short sentence prayers a prayer for the whole people; and an eminent New England divine proposed the words "O Lord, bless our nation." Accepted one afternoon on the spur of the moment, the sentence was brought up next day for reconsideration, when so many objections were raised by the laity to the word "nation" as importing too definite a recognition of national unity, that it was dropped, and instead there were adopted the words "O Lord, bless these United States."[21]

Common usage recognized this pluralistic sense. Up to the Civil War, the standard usage was, "The United States are"; after that, it became a singular noun, "The United States is," although the earlier usage persisted to the end of the century. *Congress* was likewise a plural noun, even Hamilton stating "Congress are." The change began with the aftermath of the Civil War. We are told that "Union had been preserved, but only in the narrow sense of territorial integrity had the old Union been restored. The original Federal Union had disappeared, and in its place arose a strong national state, federal chiefly in administrative machinery."[22]

The change, however, was not so marked. The double constitutionalism, legal and structural, continued to protect federalism. Even in recent years,

20. Gottfried Dietze, *The Federalist, A Classic on Federalism and Free Government* (Baltimore: Johns Hopkins Press, 1961), vii.
21. James Bryce, *The American Commonwealth* (1894). See chap 11, "The Nation and the States."
22. Samuel Eliot Morison and Henry Steele Commager, *The Growth of the American Republic*, vol. 11, fourth edition (New York: Oxford University Press, 1954), 2.

with legal constitutionalism treated as a dead letter, the structural constitutionalism continued to give resistance.[23]

The U.S. Constitution was a development of the most conservative elements in colonial history. Its roots were deeply feudal. In Europe, the dead trappings of feudalism long remained, and in many areas still survive, without any of its significance. America, more rebellious against "traditions and trappings," has maintained some of the achievements of feudalism without being past-bound. The American impatience with traditionalism has been interpreted wrongly as rootlessness. The United States is a surer heir of English liberties than England, and more deeply rooted in the Christian West than Europe itself.

The American Revolution was thus in a very far-reaching sense "a conservative counter-revolution." It was this from the foundation of the colonies. "Except for a few minor innovations designed to adjust colonial custom and experience to the immediate political and economic milieu, the Constitution contained no provisions that were new to Americans. The one radical feature of the Constitution was that it created a general government to replace the Congress of the Confederation."[24]

Limited government and constitutionalism were basic aspects of colonial faith and life, and common pulpit themes, so that Baldwin could conclude, "The constitutional convention and the written constitution were the children of the pulpit."[25]

The American political system, thus, is, first, a development of Christian feudalism, with, as shall be noted, Reformation concepts. Second, it is therefore markedly different from the doctrines of John Locke, Whig politics, and the political faith of the Enlightenment. Third, while rooted in the English tradition, it represented a new development in political and constitutional theory.

[23.] For a study of legal bypassing of constitutionalism from Theodore Roosevelt to Wilson, see John W. Burgess, *Recent Changes in American Constitutional Theory* (New York: Columbia University Press, 1923).

[24.] Forrest McDonald, *We The People, The Economic Origins of the Constitution* (Chicago: University of Chicago Press, 1958), 416. For an informative analysis and survey of the recent historical studies in the relationship of American colonial experience to the Revolution, see also Bernard Bailyn, "Political Experience and Enlightenment Ideas in Eighteenth-Century America," *The American Historical Review*, 67, no. 2 (January 1962), 339-351.

[25.] Alice M. Baldwin, *The New England Clergy and the American Revolution* (New York: Ungar, 1958), 134.

3

Legality and Revolution

A sharp point of difference between the American and French Revolutions is the question of legality and respect for law. In France, various subversive groups worked to produce chaos and anarchy, striving to effect a breakdown of law so that they might profit thereby. Hoodlums and whores were paid to incite mob action.[1]

In America, although lawlessness did occur, the leaders of the cause generally opposed it, and historians of the Tory party have noted that, despite the real hardships which the loyalists suffered, the violence was surprisingly limited in view of the circumstances. The so-called "Boston Massacre" of 1770 was used by some to incite public feeling, but it is significant that many responsible men were out of sympathy with the rioters, and two very popular leaders, John Adams and Josiah Quincy, defended the soldiers so ably that all were acquitted save two, convicted of manslaughter and only slightly punished. Later, John Adams recorded his dismay at realizing that unprincipled men, like a horse-jockey whose attorney he had sometimes been, welcomed the Revolution because of the temporary legal confusion it created. He expressed his horror at the thought that such men, seeking an escape from law rather than its surer establishment, might gain power. "If the power of the country should get into such hands, and there is great danger that it will, to what purpose have we sacrificed our time, health, and everything else? Surely we must guard against this spirit and these principles, or we shall repent of all our

---

[1] Nesta H. Webster, *The French Revolution, A Study in Democracy* (London: Constable, 1921), 39ff., 52ff., 145ff., cf. 321.

conduct." Against this, Adams placed his hope in the character of most Americans, and in God.[2]

The question of legality was an important one to colonial Americans, but their spirit was not one of barren legalism but a concern over establishing a righteous cause by righteous means. The Westminster Confession of Faith, in its chapter on "Of the Civil Magistrate," in common with other religious affirmations on the subject, made civil obedience a Christian duty. Both obedience and disobedience had to be grounded on fundamental law, on God's law, and anything else was sin. Legality was thus a necessity, since it had reference to both civil law and God's law. New England theology in the seventeenth century formulated "the central principle of the American Revolution—rebellion against an unlawful act is not rebellion but the maintenance of law."[3]

The American Revolutionists were by no means perfect men, nor was their cause at all times waged in conformity to principle. But the principles were nonetheless real and on the whole determinative. They were thus, on the one hand, opposed to the deliberate disruption of law and order which later characterized France, and, on the other hand, equally hostile to the temper apparent today in oft repeated assertions that, because the Supreme Court of the United States has spoken, good citizens have no alternative but to obey. Both attitudes were anathema to them and seen as hostile to the spirit of law. The doctrine of interposition has long legal and religious roots in American history. The doctrine of interposition was advocated by Thomas Jefferson and others as a necessary aspect of federalism, whereby a department of a particular state could prevent the invasion of the reserved powers of state and people by some department of the federal government. In terms of this framework, the federal government was prevented from being the sole determiner of its legality and legitimacy in particular contexts. Although today federal courts do not recognize interposition, it has prerevolutionary legal roots and a long and successful history since the adoption of the Constitution.[4]

[2.] John Adams, *Works*, vol. II (Boston: Little, Brown, 1865), 420-1.

[3.] Andrew C. McLaughlin, *Foundations of American Constitutionalism* (New York: Fawcett, 1961), 119. For Madison's similar views, see Gottfried Dietze, *The Federalist* (Baltimore: Johns Hopkins Press, 1961), 281f.

[4.] For its history, see James Jackson Kilpatrick, *The Sovereign States* (Chicago: Regnery, 1957).

Important in this context of legality of revolution was the influence of *Vindiciae Contra Tyrranos* (1579), held by John Adams to be one of the most influential books in America on the eve of the Revolution.[5] *Vindiciae Contra Tyrranos* held, among other things, to these doctrines: First, any ruler who commands anything contrary to the law of God thereby forfeits his realm. Second, rebellion is refusal to obey God, for we ought to obey God rather than man. To obey the ruler when he commands that which is against God's law is thus truly rebellion.[6] Third, since God's law is the fundamental law and the only true source of law, and neither king nor subject is exempt from it, war is sometimes required in order to defend God's law against the ruler. A fourth tenet also characterized this position: legal rebellion required the leadership of lesser magistrates to oppose, *in the name of the law*, the royal dissolution or contempt of law. All these doctrines were basic to the colonial cause.

The legality of the colonial cause was thus staunchly affirmed. William Henry Drayton, in reviewing the early constitutional history of South Carolina, declared king and Parliament to be the lawbreakers (May, 1776). He saw the parallel between James II in 1688 and George III in 1776. The Convention Parliament had in 1689 declared the throne to be vacant because of James' violations of office. Because of like violations, the throne of the American colonies was now also vacant, according to Drayton. The Convention Parliament charged James II with breach of "contract," i.e., declared him to be a feudal, not an absolute, monarch: James II, "having endeavored to subvert the constitution of the kingdom by breaking the original contract between king and people, and having, by the advice of

---

[5.] It is revelatory of modern historiography that the role of *Vindiciae Contra Tyrranos* is rarely mentioned, whereas Thomas Paine's works always are, in accounts of the American Revolution. The reason is obvious: *Vindiciae* is thoroughly Calvinistic; Paine is anti-Christian and a part of the intellectual milieu of the French Revolution and of the modern university. And, for purposes of the liberal midrash of history, the former is not acceptable. Paine arrived in America in December, 1774; the First Continental Congress had assembled in Carpenters' Hall, Philadelphia, September, 1774. With numerous other writers, he shared a temporary popularity. Paine's political hopes were realized in France, not America. On Paine's American failure, see David Hawke, *In the Midst of Revolution* (Philadelphia: University of Pennsylvania Press, 1961). Another aspect of the American myth concerns Franklin's American influence. Carl and Jessica Bridenbaugh have titled a study *Rebels and Gentlemen, Philadelphia in the Age of Franklin, 1740-1775* (1942, 1962). In those thirty-five years, how much did Franklin reside in Philadelphia? Franklin (1706-1790) first went to London in December of 1724, returning in 1726. In 1757, he went to England again, staying five years. In 1764, he returned to England, remaining until 1775. From 1776-1785, he was U.S. minister in Paris. Franklin was a skilled *diplomat*, not a *leader*. As a Philadelphia Quaker stated it, "Didst thee ever know Dr. Franklin to be in a minority?" Hawke states it clearly: Franklin was averse to finding "himself on the losing side," *In the Midst of Revolution*, 88. For the Pennsylvania situation, see Dietmar Rothermund, *The Layman's Progress, Religious and Political Experience in Colonial Pennsylvania, 1740-1770* (Philadelphia: University of Pennsylvania Press, 1961; and Vincent Buranelli, *The King and the Quaker, A Study of William Penn and James II* (Philadelphia: University of Pennsylvania Press, 1962).

Jesuits and other wicked persons, violated the fundamental laws and withdrawn himself out of the kingdom, has abdicated the government and the throne is hereby vacant." The Bill of Rights, December 16, 1689, thanked God for the deliverance of "this kingdom from popery and arbitrary power." The right to bear arms, privileged debate in parliament, and other long established rights had been set aside in violation of office by James II. The Bill of Rights defended and upheld "the true, ancient, and indubitable rights and liberties of the people of this kingdom" and cited the "dispensing with and the suspension of laws" as a just and legal grievance. The Glorious Revolution thus established legality in terms of the feudal constitution of England while claiming for Parliament royal absolutism.[7] With the first, it gave the colonies an impressive legal precedent to use in the American cause, and, with the second, it provided the colonies with the very ground of offense they themselves had suffered under. The legal basis for the American Revolution was thus strengthened, and the constitutional grounds for conflict ensured, by that revolution.

The fear of absolutism extended to both church and state. It is notable that this was the ground of much hostility to religious establishment in the colonies. Thus, in North Carolina, the Orange County constituency asked that the North Carolina Constitution disestablish the (Protestant) church and that Catholics be barred from office by legislation denying public office to any who affirmed "supremacy, ecclesiastical or civil, in any foreign power or authority to grant the Divine Pardon to any person who may violate moral duties or commit crimes injurious to the community."[8] Royal and papal prerogatives were commonly seen as essentially one, and alike to be fought, and, with Milton, many saw "new presbyter as old priest writ large." Neither Protestant nor Catholic ecclesiastical power, nor any kind of statist power, were to be tolerated; *absolutism* was decried from every quarter, and indications of it challenged.

The claim of Parliament over the colonies had been first asserted in 1649, after the execution of Charles I. Massachusetts, which had been ready to take arms rather than surrender its rights to Charles I, ignored Parliament's

---

[6.] The colonists, as one writer stated it, held "that the King was the rebel, not the Colonists." The concept of judicial review rests on the religious premise that no one should obey an ungodly or unconstitutional act, and that courts have the religious duty to pronounce such laws unlawful. See Alice M. Baldwin, *The New England Clergy and the American Revolution* (New York: Ungar, 1958), 118, 168f. In an election sermon by Samuel Cook, in 1770, it was held that "The New England Charter was not considered as an act of grace, but a compact between the sovereign and the first patentees;" see J. Wingall Thornton, *The Pulpit Of the American Revolution*, (Boston: Lothrop, 1887), 175. The implication was obvious to the Massachusetts lieutenant-governor, council, and legislature to whom Cook preached: violations of the compact could nullify it.

[7.] Charles F. Mullett, *Fundamental Law and the American Revolution, 1760-1776* (New York: Columbia University Press, 1933), 196f.

[8.] Robert Allen Rutland, *The Birth of the Bill of Rights, 1776-1791* (Chapel Hill: University of North Carolina Press, 1955), 57.

claims. In the eighteenth century, these claims to colonial power were more aggressively advanced by Parliament. In the ensuing conflict, it should be noted that, whatever the counter-claims of many in that day, the American Tories were predominantly true English Whigs. Locke's *Two Treatises of Government*, 1689, better expressed American Tory philosophy than colonial faith. The ablest American Tory statement, Rev. Samuel Seabury's (1729-1796) *Letters of a Westchester Farmer* (1774-1775), is a defense of parliamentary authority. In "The Congress Canvassed," Seabury denied the validity of any "strong and lamentable cries about liberty" since all such rights and liberties "are, in a great measure, founded" on the authority of Parliament.[9] The primary function of government is "security."[10] Attacking "American whiggism," Seabury declared that "to talk of being liege subjects of King George, while we disavow the authority of Parliament is another piece of whiggish nonsense."[11] Seabury affirmed, among other things, first, the supreme authority of Parliament as against king, people, and church. Second, he held the rights and liberties of citizens to depend "in a great measure" on acts or concessions of parliament. The state, thus, in the form of parliament, is the basic source of rights; they "ultimately depend" on Parliament.

Hamilton, who as a young man answered Seabury, summed up the colonial position later in *The Federalist:* "It is one thing to be subordinate to the laws, and another to be dependent on the legislative body" (no. 71).

The English Revolution of 1688 had established the supremacy of Parliament in church and state alike. William and Mary had sworn in their coronation oath to govern the kingdom "and the dominions thereunto belonging according to the statutes in Parliament agreed on." The colonies, however, were increasingly concerned with the immunities of the individual from the state, and, very often, from the church, and with the independence of the church. They distrusted Parliament and its claims, but they feared their own legislatures no less: they were concerned with immunities and protection from legislative and other state powers.[12] *The Federalist* recognized the right of revolution against unlawful acts of government as itself obedience to law, reflecting here *Vindiciae Contra Tyrranos*.[13] The doctrine of interposition was developed as a formal and lawful means to this end. The popularity of Montesquieu in the colonies was due to the fact that he saw, as the true constitution of English liberty,

[9.] Samuel Seabury, *Letters of a Westchester Farmer*, Publication of the Westchester County Historical Society, 8 (White Plains, N.Y.: Westchester County Historical Society, 1930), 73.
[10.] *Ibid.*, 90f.
[11.] *Ibid.*, "A View of the Controversy," 112.
[12.] Gottfied Dietze, *The Federalist, A Classic on Federalism and Free Government* (Baltimore: Johns Hopkins Press, 1961), 58, 60f., 72, 130, 157-160.
[13.] *Ibid.*, 281f.

that division and separation of powers which the colonists held to be the essence of their English tradition. The success of Montesquieu as well as many another European writer was not in influencing the colonies, but in stating at particular points what the colonists believed, enabling them now, on the basis of international authorities, to buttress their case before the nations. The roots of their conception of law were deep in English and Western Christian history, but they represented also a long colonial development. Massachusetts, for example, had refused in Cromwell's day to accept parliamentary sovereignty, and Winthrop had described clearly the implications of such authority.

John Cotton very early stated the Puritan thesis clearly, declaring it wrong to give unlimited or unconditional power or authority to any in church or state:

> It is necessary therefore, that all power on earth be limited, Church power or other....It is counted a matter of danger to the State to limit Prerogatives; but it is a further danger, not to have them limited....It is therefore fit for every man to be studious of the bounds which the Lord hath set: and for the People, in whom fundamentally all power lyes, to give as much power as God in his word gives to men: and it is meet that Magistrates in the Commonwealth, and so officers in Churches should desire to know the utmost bounds of their own power, and it is safe for both: All entrenchment upon the bounds which God hath not given, they are not enlargements, but burdens and snare[14]

Any and every order of society, being made up of sinful men, will seek to exploit its potential powers to the limit and must therefore be carefully restrained. As Cotton grimly stated it, "If you tether a Beast at night, he knows the length of his tether before morning."[15]

Tocqueville was aware of the marked difference between England and America at this point. In the United States, legislative absolutism was denied, as well as the finality of positive law. In England, to the contrary, according to Delolme, "It is a fundamental principle with the English lawyers, that parliament can do everything except making a woman a man, or a man a woman." Tocqueville also cited Blackstone on "the power and jurisdiction of parliament" as "transcendant and absolute...sovereign and uncontrollable authority...ecclesiastical and temporal...absolute despotic power...It can, in short, do everything that is not naturally impossible to be done; and, therefore, some have not scrupled to call its power, by a figure rather too bold, the omnipotence of parliament."[16] The powers

---

[14.] John Cotton, *An Exposition upon the Thirteenth Chapter of the Revelation* (London, 1655), 72. See also Perry Miller, ed., *The American Puritans, Their Prose and Poetry* (Garden City, N. Y.: Doubleday Anchor, 1956), 84-88.

[15.] Cotton, *Thirteenth Chapter of Revelation*, 72.

[16.] Alexis de Tocqueville, *Democracy in America*, vol. I (New York: Langley, 1841), 104, 490f.

claimed by the English Parliament, from the American view, might be acceptable to England, but the colonies had their own parliaments or assemblies and their own constitutional histories.

Two legal traditions were thus in conflict. Both had ancient roots. And the colonies were right in affirming that their tradition constituted what was known as English liberty and the rights of Englishmen; they were the truer heirs and developers of that body of doctrine and law. In terms of that legal inheritance, the Declaration of Independence was signed by the representatives of the constituent states in the Continental Congress. Parliamentary power was implicitly denied and the king declared guilty of breach of contract.

In 1779, Congress reviewed the legal documents involved and declared its course to be the legal one in its *Observations on the American Revolution.*[17] It was affirmed, on the basis of these things, that the colonies were connected with England only in having a common prince, and also that the Revolution of 1688 had confirmed the right of revolution on breach of contract.

> And it being evident that the two countries not only had not, but really could not have (on free principles) any political connection but thro' the prince — so that exercised in the revolution of England demonstrated since, and generally admitted, must necessarily draw with it the right to independence, which is above stated.[18]

Justice was thus on the side of the colonies. Parliament's position was implicitly illegal: *power invalid in the king did not become valid in Parliament's hands, being fundamentally invalid.* Absolutism in the king had been rejected as an invalid concept in the English Revolution and the Glorious Revolution. How could Parliament validly appropriate an already invalid power? The American Revolution was thus legal, and it was a move to reestablish law, and illegality and its onus rested on king and Parliament.

The difference between the American and French Revolutions is again a marked one. In France, the revolutionists aimed at the breakdown of law and order so that they could capitalize on anarchy. Riots and mob violence were essential tools of action. In America, revolution aimed at establishing law. Hence, Edmund Burke opposed North's government almost to the point of treason, convinced that the colonists were fighting for the cause of English liberty. The defeat of the colonies, he believed, would be a defeat of the cause of liberty in England. Burke's opposition to the French Revolution was thus based on no inconsistency of thought but rather a recognition of the very different natures of the two revolutions. Many

---

[17.] Published by a Resolution of Congress, 1779. William Henry Engle, ed., *Pennsylvania Archives, Third Series,* vol. VII (Harrisburg, Penn.: State Printer, 1866), 519-623. An important although neglected document.

[18.] *Ibid.,* 523.

historians since have attempted to reinterpret the American Revolution in terms of a few radical thinkers and have accordingly charged Burke with inconsistency. Burke, however, saw the American Revolution as basically Christian and English in its origins and demands. The rootlessness Burke noted in France was absent in America. Americans were proud of their roots. When Mary Wollstonecraft, in her *French Revolution,* observed, "There is so much to destroy and almost all to create anew," John Adams was moved to comment ironically, "Joel Barlow in his History, no doubt on this principle will record Tom Paine as the greatest politician of the Revolution."[19] The irony was in order. Neither Barlow nor Paine, nor any other champions of continental and English radicalism, had any major influence on the legal development of American constitutionalism. They had concerned themselves with *abstract* rights. The colonials were concerned with a *legal* situation. As Adams observed, "The authority of parliament was never generally acknowledged in America."[20] In matters of empire, Parliament's power was recognized, but not with reference to internal policy. In speaking of *rights,* the colonists had a particular legal tradition in mind.

Again, for Burke, it was an article of faith that man is a religious creature; as a result, the state or government of man must also reflect that religious faith. Burke's political theory was thus, in Mahoney's words, a "basically Christian conception of the state."[21] Religion is the basis of civil society. Burke saw the American Revolution as a variant of the English Christian concept of society and government seeking to gain its logical development. In America, from "six capital sources,—of descent, of form of government, of religion in the northern provinces, of manners in the southern, of education, of remoteness of situation from the first mover of government, — from all of these causes a fierce spirit of liberty has grown up." To fight America, England, warned Burke, would be fighting itself: "For in order to prove that the Americans have no right to their liberties, we are every day endeavoring to subvert the maxims which preserve the whole spirit of our own."[22] Americans also saw their cause not only as a defense of their own liberties but the protection of Englishmen at home from the destruction of their liberties. Thus a pamphlet, *The Crisis,* June, 1754, attributed to Rev. Samuel Cooper, held that the destruction of American liberty by parliamentary usurpation ultimately involved the destruction of the

---

19. Zoltan Haraszti, *John Adams and the Prophets of Progress* (Cambridge, Mass.: Harvard University Press, 1952), 204.
20. *Works,* vol. IV, 47.
21. Thomas H. D. Mahoney, introduction to Edmund Burke, *Reflections on the Revolution in France* (Indianapolis: Bobbs-Merrill, 1955), xxiv. For Burke's development of this argument, see 102f.
22. Edmund Burke, "Conciliation with America," 1775; *Old South Leaflets,* 8, no. 176-200 (Boston: Old South Meeting House, n. d.), 13, 15, 489.

essence of liberty in the homeland. This pamphlet was reprinted in London
in 1776 as *The Crisis, or a Full Defense of the Colonies.*[23]

Almost a decade prior to Burke's statement of the case, the colonial cause
had to a large measure been recognized as valid in Parliament in Lord
Chatham's "speech on the Stamp Act," January 14, 1766:

> The Commoners of America, represented in their several assemblies,
> have ever been in possession of the exercise of this their constitutional
> right, of giving and granting their own money. They would have been
> slaves if they had not enjoyed it. At the same time this kingdom, as the
> supreme governing and legislative power, has always bound the
> colonies by her laws, by her regulations and restrictions in trade, in
> navigation, in manufactures—in everything except that of taking their
> money out of their pockets without their consent.[24]

Such legal distinctions between internal and imperial legislation may seem
legal hairsplitting to another era, but, granted that at many points the
distinction is difficult, it does not cease for that matter to be valid. For many
Americans, liberty depended upon it.

At a later date, Americans defended not only the legality of their cause
but also its value to England as well. As Robert C. Winthrop declared in
"The Centennial of Independence," Boston, July 4, 1876, "We did unite and
persevere. We did prevail and triumph. And it is hardly too much to say
that we did 'save England.' We saved her from herself; — saved her from
being the successful instrument of overthrowing the rights of
Englishmen."[25]

Finally, one of the revealing facts concerning the revolutionary era is
that the sale of English law books, Blackstone and Coke in particular, was
very great in the colonies, nearly 2500 copies of Blackstone's *Commentaries*
having been sold in the ten years prior to the Revolution. This was not
surprising: legality and the law were of major concern to the colonists.
And, while Blackstone's doctrine of the omnipotence of Parliament was
not always to their taste, the colonial thinkers were concerned with an
understanding of law, and with legality. Coke accordingly gained "more
veneration in America than England" because of his hostility to the concept
of legal sovereignty.

But, basic to all colonial thought, was the ancient and Christian sense of
the transcendence and majesty of law. According to John Calvin, "the law
is a silent magistrate, and a magistrate a speaking law."[26] In terms of the
authority of this silent magistrate, the rebelling colonials moved, and in
terms of this faith, their magistrates became speaking laws. Constitu-

---

[23.] Baldwin, *New England Clergy and the American Revolution,* 85.
[24.] *Old South Leaflet,* no. 199, 4, 452.
[25.] *Old South Leaflet,* no., 191, 15, 303.
[26.] *Institutes,* IV,14, 20.

tionalism, for the colonials, meant, as Baldwin has demonstrated with reference to the New England clergy, the absolute and sovereign God and His law undergirding the silent magistrate and the speaking law.

4

Sovereignty

The doctrine of parliamentary sovereignty and absolutism was fought by the American Revolution as legally and morally wrong. Although some references to *popular* sovereignty are to be found in the constitutional records, these statements have reference to political sovereignty.[1] *Legal* sovereignty was definitely denied, and the people themselves, although granted suffrage, were distrusted. In this distrust no aristocratic temper was displayed: there was a distrust of all classes, and a feeling that restraints upon the power of all were necessary. The background to this distrust of sovereignty was both early medieval and Calvinist. Political Calvinism had affirmed, as its battle-cry, such statements as "The Crown Rights of King Jesus," and "To God alone belongs dominion."

The Christian, Western tradition in America was hostile to the doctrine of sovereignty and affirmed, with reference to the civil order, the doctrine of *limited power*. This meant, first, a *division* of powers, which naturally implied, second, a *multiplicity* of powers, and, third, a *complexity* of powers. Statism strives continually for a simplicity of government, assuming that the complexity of life is amenable to the mind of the planner and governor. John Adams noted this difference. When Mary Wollstonecraft wrote, "It will be allowed by every humane and considerate being that a political

---

[1.] M. J. C. Vile, *The Structure of American Federalism* (New York: Oxford University Press, 1961), 25f. Vile speaks of divided sovereignty of government in the United States and cites *The Federalist* (no. 62) with reference to "the residual sovereignty of the States." The reference in *The Federalist* is to political, not legal, sovereignty. Most references to the idea of sovereignty in *The Federalist* are historical, referring to Hellenic and European Confederations, and the Articles of Confederation.

system more simple than has hitherto existed would effectually check those
aspiring follies, which have banished from governments the very shadow
of justice and magnanimity," Adams commented, "There can be none more
simple than despotism. The triple complication, not simplicity, is to be
sought for." After observations on Miss Wollstonecraft's character, Adams
added:

> The word "simplicity" in the course of seven years has murdered its
> millions—and produced more horrors than monarchy did in a century.
> A woman would be more simple if she had but one eye or one breast;
> yet nature chose she should have two as more convenient as well as
> ornamental. A man would be more simple with but one ear, one arm,
> one leg. Shall a legislature have but one chamber then, merely because
> it is more simple? A wagon would be more simple if it went upon one
> wheel: yet no art could prevent it from oversetting at every step.[2]

Adams held to original sin as basic to Christianity, and he trusted no group
accordingly.[3] In religion Adams was Arminian,[4] but in politics Augustinian
and Calvinist.[5] Together with his theological Arminianism, he reflected at
many points philosophical Calvinism, giving priority to the doctrine of
creation and of man's analogical knowledge even in his dissent.[6]

This respect for the complexity of life had more than Calvinistic roots.
It was deeply imbedded in the Augustinian and feudal inheritance of the
colonists. Note, for example, the complicated feudal responsibilities of
John of Toul:

> I, John of Toul, make known that I am the liege man of the Lady
> Beatrice, Countess of Troyes, and of her son Theobald, Count of
> Champagne, against every creature, living or dead, saving my
> allegiance to Lord Enjorand of Coucy, Lord of Arcis, and the Count
> of Grandpre. If it should happen that the Count of Grandpre should
> be at war with the countess and count of Champagne in his own
> quarrel, I will aid the Count of Grandpre in my own person, and will
> send to the Count and the Countess of Champagne the knights whose
> service I owe to them for the fief which I hold of them. But if the
> Count of Grandpre shall make war on the Countess and the Count of
> Champagne on behalf of his friends and not in his own quarrel, I will
> aid in my own person the Countess and Count of Champagne, and
> will send one knight to the Count of Grandpre for the service which
> I owe him for the fief which I hold of him, but I will not go myself
> into the territory of the Count of Grandpre to make war on him.[7]

[2.] Zoltan Haraszti, *John Adams and the Prophets of Progress* (Cambridge, Mass.: Harvard University Press, 1952), 233f.
[3.] *Ibid.*, 24, 187.
[4.] John Adams, *Works*, vol. I (Boston: Little, Brown, 1865), 36f., 39f.
[5.] *Ibid.*, 426-28.
[6.] Haraszti, 297f.
[7.] James Westfall Thompson and Edgar Nathaniel Johnson, *An Introduction to Medieval Europe, 300-1500* (New York: Norton, 1937), 302.

This certainly involved a complexity of relationships and responsibilities, and the possibility of conflict and tension. But life is not made easier but rather more difficult by the relegation of responsibility to the state. Responsibility requires complexity. And self-government is an assumption of responsibility in the face of life's complexity and problems. In civil government, complexity of structure with a division and limitation of powers is the essence of responsible government and basic to liberty.

In terms of this inheritance, sovereignty was an alien concept on the colonial and constitutional scene. As Murray has noted:

> Nowhere in the American structure is there accumulated the plenitude of legal sovereignty possessed in England by the Queen in Parliament. In fact, the term "legal sovereignty" makes no sense in America, where sovereignty (if the alien term must be used) is purely political. The United States has a government, or better, a structure of governments operating on different levels. The American state has no sovereignty in the classic Continental sense.[8]

A telling analysis of this has been made by A. F. Pollard, who has called attention to this distinctive aspect of the American political tradition:

> The colonies had been as anxious to get rid of James II in 1688 as they were to be free from Parliament in 1776. Their fundamental objection was to any sovereignty vested in any State whatsoever even in their own. Americans may be defined as that part of the English-speaking world which has instinctively revolted against the doctrine of the sovereignty of the State and has, not quite successfully, striven to maintain that attitude from the time of the Pilgrim Fathers to the present day....It is this denial of all sovereignty which gives its profound and permanent interest to the American Revolution. The Pilgrim Fathers crossed the Atlantic to escape from sovereign power; Washington called it a "monster"; the Professor of American History at Oxford calls it a "bugaboo"...and Mr. Lansing writes of the Peace Conference that "nine-tenths of all international difficulties arise out of the problem of sovereignty and the so-called sovereign state."[9]

This anti-sovereignty doctrine, medieval in origin and Puritan in development, was transplanted from England to America. The Boston Tea Party was "the burial...of the sovereignty of the State so far as America was concerned." The English Middle Ages had no political sovereignty, and Americans moved in terms of that tradition; "medieval English history is more theirs than the periods in which they had a separate history of their own; and instinctive memory has much to do with political thought and with the writing of history." The colonists, with regard to taxation, law,

---

[8] John Courtney Murray, S.J., *We Hold These Truths* (New York: Sheed and Ward, 1960), 70.
[9] A. F. Pollard, *Factors in American History* (New York: Macmillan, 1925), 33f.

and constitution, wanted "a mediaeval restoration" in which "each estate or state made its own grant and was bound by that alone."[10]

The doctrine of sovereignty was not a part of constitutional theory, which *assumed* the higher law framework and structurally eliminated legal sovereignty. The doctrine was, however, gradually reintroduced into American thought through the influence of Blackstone on lawyers.[11] The 11th Amendment, 1798, was an assertion of state sovereignty as against the right of men in other states to sue for justice.[12] This doctrine has since then been under steady attack and was in 1962 overthrown in California in its non-constitutional aspect, i.e., with reference to suits by citizens of the state.[13] The next great breach after the 11th Amendment came when Congress, in 1862, by a legislative rather than constitutional measure, abolished slavery in the territories. Lincoln, in abolishing slavery in the rebellious states, recognized the unconstitutionality of his step but undertook it nonetheless. It was an assertion of national and imperial supremacy and sovereignty.[14] The 14th Amendment, illegally ratified,[15] provided grounds for the interference of the federal government in the jurisdiction of state governments. These implications of the 14th Amendment were progressively utilized by the Supreme Court shortly after the beginning of the twentieth century, and there began the court's recession from its conception of America as a Christian country and its development of the thesis of a unitary State. As the court embraced moral relativism as its religious principle, so it established national sovereignty and absolutism as a corollary to its denial of higher law. When Chief Justice Vinson, after World War II, asserted, "Nothing is more certain in modern society than the principle that there are no absolutes," it was a corollary to the Supreme Court's assertion of absolutism and a denial of any appeal beyond itself. Not surprisingly, Eisenhower and Kennedy, two presidents dedicated to the same philosophy, urged full obedience to Supreme Court decisions as *the law*.

[10.] *Ibid.*, 35, 39, 41.

[11.] Edward S. Corwin, *The "Higher Law" Background of American Constitutional Law* (Ithaca, N. Y.: Great Seal Books, Cornell, 1955), 84-9.

[12.] Pollard, 121. J. J. Kilpatrick, *The Sovereign States*, 51-58, gives an able defense of the 11th Amendment. In this context, note an important comment by Kilpatrick, "the States delegated — not surrendered, but *delegated* — only certain of their powers (to the Constitution), retaining all others to themselves."

[13.] "State in Negligence Suit Trap," and "Divine Right of State Overthrown," *Oakland Tribune*, 5 August 1962, 1-2. The California Legislature in 1963 overruled the court; See "Signs Bills Limiting State Liability Suits," *Tribune* (Redwood City, Calif.), 18 July 1963, 17,

[14.] Pollard, 189f.

[15.] See Walter E. Long, *The Fourteenth Amendment to the Constitution of the United States, A Study* (Austin, Texas: No. 1 Green Lanes, P. O. Box 1, 1960). See also Felix Morley, *Freedom and Federalism* (Chicago: Regnery, 1959), 68-71. A very careful analysis has also been made by *The Dan Smoot Report*, 9, no. 1 (7 January 1963), 1-8.

But the justification of the Revolution had not been a Declaration of Sovereignty but of Independence. The Constitution established neither a confederation nor a national state, but rather a federal union. Its conception of power was Christian: power is *ministerial, not legislative, i.e.,* powers in any area, church, state, school, or family, are not endowed with ability to create laws apart from the higher law but only to administer fundamental law as man is able to grasp and approximate it. Civil government is thus an administrator rather than a creator of law; it is not sovereign over law but is under law. The doctrine of express powers is a strong limitation on even the administrative or ministerial role of civil government and is not explicable except in terms of the Christian philosophical development which in Chalcedon sundered the divine-human bond as it appeared in the state and relegated to the human order a ministerial function.

The issues involved in the Revolution and Constitution were sharply stated on April 30, 1839, by John Quincy Adams, speaking in New York on "The Jubilee of the Constitution." Speaking of the revolutionists, Adams declared, "English liberties had failed them. From the omnipotence of Parliament the colonists appealed to the rights of man and the omnipotence of the God of battles."[16] Adams saw the Revolution and the continuing history of the United States as a battle against majoritarianism and the doctrine of sovereignty. Three forces had thus far arrayed themselves *against* the American faith and *for* sovereignty. The first, in the Revolution and the events leading to it, was the doctrine of "the omnipotence of the British Parliament."[17] Second, the United States under the Articles of Confederation again faced the threat of sovereignty. The Articles declared, "Each State retains its sovereignty." Asked Adams,

> Where did each state get the sovereignty which it retains? In the Declaration of Independence the delegates of the colonies in Congress assembled, in the name and by the authority of the good people of the colonies, declare, not each colony, but the United Colonies, in fact, and of right, not sovereign, but free and independent states.[18]

Third, the South, to justify its position with reference to slavery, turned aside from constitutional ideas to "the irresponsible despotism of state sovereignty."[19] It could be added, of course, that subsequently the radical Republicans tried to answer the South with the equally irresponsible despotism of national sovereignty. Against this concept of sovereignty, Adams held, both the Declaration of Independence and the Constitution

[16.] Selim H. Peabody, ed., *American Patriotism, Speeches, Letters, and other Papers which illustrate the Foundation, the Development, the Preservation of the United States of America* (New York: American Book Exchange, 1880), 313.

[17.] *Ibid.*

[18.] *Ibid.*, 318.

[19.] *Ibid.*, 319.

stood firm, having been the result of active military and philosophical battle against it.

> There is the Declaration of Independence, and there is the Constitution of the United States—let them speak for themselves. The grossly immoral and dishonest doctrine of despotic state sovereignty, the exclusive judge of its own obligations, and responsible to no power on earth or in heaven, for the violation of them, is not there. The Declaration says it is not in me. The Constitution says it is not in me.[20]

It should be noted that Adams, in opposing the idea of sovereignty, insisted on the necessity of a double responsibility in civil government, to "earth," i.e., society, and to "heaven" or God. Responsibility connotes subordination; we are under those to whom we are responsible. An irresponsible man is one under authority who denies or abuses that responsibility. God, however, is beyond the category of responsibility, being under no man nor under any law, but rather totally self-sufficient. The aseity or self-derived being of God places Him beyond all such circumscription. Man, however, and civil government are and must be responsible agencies. If the transcendental responsibility, the subordination to God, be removed, then man becomes a creature of the state and responsible to it, and the aseity or self-derived being of the state is asserted. Such a man may fear the State and its power, but, by virtue of his relativism or naturalism, no effective and transcendental appeal exists.

In this context, the assertions of three presidents prior to their election are of significance. According to Franklin Delano Roosevelt:

> As a matter of fact and law, the governing rights of the states are any of those which have not been surrendered to the National Government by the Constitution or its amendments. Wisely or unwisely, people know that under the 18th Amendment Congress has been given the right to legislate on this particular subject, but this is not the case in the matter of a great number of other vital problems of government, such as the conduct of public utilities, of banks, of insurance, of business, of agriculture, of education, of social welfare, and of a dozen other important features. In these, Washington must never be permitted to interefere in these avenues of our affairs.... Now, to bring about government by oligarchy masquerading as democracy, it is fundamentally essential that practically all authority and control be centralized in our National Government.[21]

[20.] *Ibid.*, 321. Adams held Locke in respect, it should be noted, in terms of this faith. The defense of English liberties by Locke endeared him to Americans. Moreover, Locke had, despite his majoritarianism, a strong adherence to feudalism; his proposed colonial constitution was a recreation of feudalism.

[21.] "Radio Address on State's Rights," March 2, 1930, *The Public Papers and Addresses of Franklin D. Roosevelt*, vol. I, *The Genesis of the New Deal, 1928-1932*, (New York: Random House, 1938), 569-575. See also, "Roosevelt Decries Waning State Rule," *New York Times*, 3 March 1930, 1.

Dwight D. Eisenhower seemed to echo Washington's warning ("Government is not reason, it is not eloquence—it is a force. Like fire, it is a dangerous servant and a fearful master") when he concluded:

> Every step we take toward making the State the caretaker of our lives, by that much we move toward making the State our master.

Again, while still a senator, John F. Kennedy declared on April 23, 1950:

> The scarlet thread running thru the thoughts and actions of people all over the world is the delegation of great problems to the all-absorbing leviathan—the state.... Every time that we try to lift a problem to the government, to the same extent we are sacrificing the liberties of the people.

There is no reason to doubt the sincerity of these statements, nor their impotence. All three men laid claims to being professing Christians, and yet all three clearly saw the state as the order of salvation and acted accordingly. They revealed no awareness of the implications of Chalcedon for political science, nor of the transcendental responsibility of governments. While they feared statism and its doctrine of sovereignty, they only furthered it. If man has no hope beyond the state, no fear of that state can deliver him from its hands. The colonial denial of sovereignty was an aspect of the Christian faith of the day; the revival of the doctrine of sovereignty and its increasingly menacing assertion is a product of the decline of theological Christianity and the rise of relativism, naturalism, and man-centered (anthropological) social-gospel Christianity.

5

The Right to Emigrate

The right to emigrate is not normally conceived of as a right, but, in terms of the American constitutional background, it has an important status as a right.

The Puritans saw themselves as pilgrims and sojourners like Abraham, their destination and citizenship being in that city whose builder and maker is God. Emigration in terms of this faith made them the moving force in the colonies. Not only did Puritans settle directly in virtually every colony, but many moved southward in protests against various New England policies or injustices. The faith that made them unyielding in New England made them aggressively missionary-minded in their new homes. Again, New England provided the ships and seamen for America, and these, as they docked in Virginia or the Carolinas, were outspoken in declaring their political and religious faith. Because of this, some colonial governors came to regard New England seamen as pestilential fellows. Furthermore, New England, and Massachusetts in particular, early took the lead in developing the implications of its faith, probing philosophically, religiously, and politically into the issues of church, state, and faith, and so exercised an influence on the laws and constitutions of the various colonies and states.

A brief glance at the Old Testament commonwealth is necessary to an understanding of this right to emigrate. To the modern mind, the Mosaic law involved strange paradoxes. It required death for *proselyting* to an alien faith but did not legally require the tithe. Inward faith was not compelled, but an outward adherence to the covenant could not be subverted without treason. Israel was a covenant people; to remain within the covenant and then subvert it was treason deserving death. They were a people established in terms of Abraham's migration, and Moses' migration with the people, and the land was the land of the covenant. Each generation either confirmed the covenant or departed from it. Entrance into the covenant was not compulsory (2 Chron. 29), but the privileges of the covenant and the covenant land were reserved to the faithful. The climax of apostasy was hence expulsion. This, of course, was the thesis of Michael Wigglesworth's poem, *God's Controversy with New England*. The beginnings made by the Christian pilgrims and sojourners had been godly:

> God's throne was here set up, here was
>   His tabernacle pight;
> This was the place and these the folk
>   In whom He took delight.

But let New England beware of indifference towards their covenant God, who warns:

> Except you seriously, and soon, repent,
>   I'll not delay your pain and heavy punishment.

Massachusetts was established as a covenant people. Every sphere of life involved either a covenant or covenant activity. Thus, John Davenport spoke of "National, Conjugal, Social," and other covenants. Three covenants in particular are to be noted as basic to an understanding of the Massachusetts Bay Colony:

1. The church covenant
2. The civil covenant
3. The personal covenant

The personal covenant was basic, in that it involved the relationship of the individual to God through Christ. All men were either covenant-keepers or covenant-breakers, having been created covenant men in Adam. For a covenant people, there was no entrance into the full life of church or state, or suffrage in them, without *mature* evidence of *membership and responsibility* in the personal covenant. The fact that few voted, and church membership was limited (both then and well after the Revolution), did not mean that few were considered Christians. Rather, at the beginning, and even later, all or virtually all were assumed to be Christian, although many were regarded as babes in Christ in terms of maturity of faith. The limitation was twofold: church and state were fearful of immature Christians being lightly given full membership, and individuals were hesitant about assuming mature responsibility, regarded by them as awesome, without much soul-searching. At times men had to be urged to assume responsibilities for which religious and civil authorities deemed them ready. Those not in full communion were assumed to be Christian, and their children also. In Wigglesworth's words, "For Christian's children are an holy seed." Thus, in a very real sense, the presuppositions of the Half-Way Covenant were early present in New England, although applied in a different sense. The distinction, however, was only a version of the ancient distinction between catechumens and baptized, with this notable difference: baptism was now presupposed for both classes as within the covenant, and communion reserved. It was basic that the people were a covenant people, and the colony a covenant colony of the City of God.

This idea of a covenant people, while most prominent in New England, was common to the colonies and to their English background. The basic nature of the Puritan army in England, despite its variety of theological emphases, was its covenanted basis. "The *Solemn Engagement of the Army* was a contract of voluntary association, a covenant among the soldiers, with the nation, and before God."[1] The language of covenant or compact influenced civil and ecclesiastical polity. As Tocqueville observed much later, "In the United States the sovereign authority is religious."[2] *Constitutionalism is a form of covenantalism,* and it requires for stability the vitality of the personal covenant to supply health and character on the part of the people. Attempts to transport constitutionalism, as to South America, the Mexican Constitution of 1824 (a copy of the U.S. Constitution), and to the African states, have resulted in futility. Without the conception of the personal covenant of grace, the civil covenant and constitution is rootless and quickly becomes invalid.

Covenantalism saw its origin in the emigrant Abraham, and the emigrant people under Moses who left Egypt, the house of bondage, for Canaan, the land of promise. Such a people were the colonial Americans, as preachers of all churches and colonies reminded them, and as the colonists reminded themselves. American history can be described as "the American pilgrimage." Freud could declare, in *Beyond the Pleasure Principle* (1922), that "the goal of all life is death...Life is but the circuitous route to death." But Americans could believe that they had been led to a promised land which was a figure or type, as was Canaan, of their true city or land, the eternal Kingdom of God. Isaac Watts' *Jordan* declared:

> There is a land of pure delight where saints immortal reign...
> Sweet fields beyond the swelling flood stand dress'd in living green
> So to the Jews old Canaan stood while Jordan roll'd between.

Other hymns written in or popular in America celebrated the same faith: "Shall we gather at the river?," "I'm bound for the land of Canaan," "I'm just a poor wayfaring stranger, "Deep River," and the like. The nineteenth

---

[1.] A.S.P. Woodhouse, ed., *Puritanism and Liberty* (London: Dent, 1938), 75.
[2.] Alexis de Tocqueville, *Democracy in America*, vol. I, (New York: Langley, 1841), 332.

century saw even more hymns expressing this faith.[3] Many hymns exulted
in the attainment of the promise by faith:

> I've reached the land of corn and wine
> And all its riches freely mine.

This exultant note is characteristically American Christianity: the
struggling, suffering, but exultantly triumphant pilgrim.

Emigration then was *basic* to covenantalism, and, with emigration, the
right to establish a godly society and institutions in terms of that faith.
Thus, the right to emigrate, and to establish then a new covenanted body,
was basic to this faith. The freedom not to contract or covenant was
recognized, which meant separation in terms of that dissent. There was
thus the right to leave the jurisdiction of contract or covenant, but not the
right to breach of contract, which constituted subversion and apostasy. The
problem with Roger Williams and the Quakers was their insistence on
trying to subvert the covenant rather than establishing their own.
Covenantalism strongly emphasized liberty of conscience, but it was not
the anarchistic interpretation common to the twentieth century. Thus,
according to the Westminster Confession of Faith, Chapter XX, "God
alone is lord of the conscience, and hath left it free from the doctrines and
commandments of men which are in any thing contrary to his Word, or
beside it, in matters of faith or worship. So that to believe such doctrines,
or to obey such commandments out of conscience, is to betray true liberty
of conscience; and the requiring of an implicit faith, and an absolute and
blind obedience, is to destroy liberty of conscience, and reason also." The
Christian conscience is responsible to God; the humanistic conscience has
no transcendental responsibility but answers only to itself or any
self-established norm it pleases. The Christian conscience is ready to wage
war on the state and be a pilgrim in terms of God and covenant; the
humanistic conscience wants the state to indulge its total license as a
personal privilege. The Christian conscience expects tension and clash with
the world and peace with God; the humanistic conscience works towards
peace with the world and independence from God. The Christian
conscience thus calls for pilgrimage throughout life and sees life as a
pilgrimage and an emigration.

The right to emigrate was cherished from the beginning in
Massachusetts. During a two-year period, because of fears of losing their
charter, fears of Indian attack, and a sense of helplessness because of limited
numbers, there was some abridgement of the right, which was later legally
secured in 1641. In 1633, the issue came up in the Newtown case. The right

---

[3.] See Cyclone Covey, *The American Pilgrimage, The Roots of American History, Religion and Culture* (New York: Colliers, 1961), 45f. Covey, in his brilliant study,
sees Plato and Augustine as Puritanism's "double fountainhead" (54). But the influence of Platonism on Puritanism was a later development.

to emigrate was denied by a majority of the magistrates but upheld by the majority of deputies to the General Court. John Cotton preached a sermon in support of the magistrates, and the matter was settled by compromise, additional lands being given to the Newtown people. Expediency thus prevailed. In 1635, Stoughton, a deputy, was punished for writing a treatise opposing the magistrate's position. However, the magistrates conceded the right to emigrate to the people of Roxbury and Watertown, but required at the same time that they remain under the jurisdiction of Massachusetts. The popular discontent with this position, so alien to their presuppositions, led in 1641 to Article 17 of the Massachusetts *Body of Liberties:*

> Every man of or within this Jurisdiction shall have free libertie, notwithstanding any Civill power to remove both himselfe, and his familie at their pleasure out of the same, provided there be no legall impediment to the contrarie.

This principle and law was widely copied, although Virginia sought to discourage such emigration. North Carolina entered it, with limitation, into its *Declaration of Rights.* Legally or practically, there was a steady acceptance of this right to emigrate, and a surrender subsequently both of claims to the contrary and of western lands to such emigration. The Northwest Ordinance of July 13, 1787, was the triumph of this principle. It forbad, not religious establishment in the new territories, but rather molestation "on account of…mode of worship, or religious sentiments" (Article I), and firmly guaranteed the civil encouragement of "religion, morality, and knowledge" (Article III). Passed again by Congress after the ratification of the Constitution *and* the Bill of Rights, the Northwest Ordinance undergirded this right to emigrate.

The right to emigrate is thus in the Constitution by virtue of its limitation to express powers only, and by virtue of the freedom to erect new states in western territories. The powers of the separate states, and the right of each state to establish or disestablish a church, made possible a concept of the right to emigrate and create new social orders within the framework. The state was thus the area of social theory and particular commitment and experimentation, and the federal government the area of unity in terms of abstinence. It is in this context that the First Amendment was written.

Clergymen in particular were hostile to ratification of the Constitution until assured that there would be no *federal* establishment of religion. Others, like John Adams, wanted *state* establishment but were equally hostile to federal establishment. The religious and political sovereignty of Parliament had been alike oppressive in the years prior to 1776, and no such authority in either realm was desired in America. Establishment in some form or another continued in some areas throughout the nineteenth century, and in New Hampshire suffrage was religiously restricted into the twentieth century. Nevertheless, very early, men like Rev. Isaac Backus opposed all religious establishments, as his *Church History of New England* makes clear, while espousing a Christian republic.

The consequence of this was the retention and development of particular cultures by the various states, with the integrity of variations within the counties also recognized, sometimes by plural establishments. The United States thus presented a genuinely and extensively pluralistic picture. To this day, half the counties in the United States are dominated by a single religious denomination, so that a particular area is Baptist, Roman Catholic, Congregational, Lutheran, etc., in character. Again, racial and national groups, German, Polish, Swedish, Armenian, Dutch, etc., have tended to colonize in particular areas, so that an extensive coincidence of religion, race, and culture prevails within the counties of the United States.

The 14th Amendment has been instrumental in undercutting the vitality of this right to emigrate and to colonize, in that it has provided grounds for federal interference in states, and the nullification of state laws embodying particular differences, religious or political. The increasing demand for uniform, federally imposed divorce, traffic, and criminal laws is hostile to the right to emigrate *and* to local authority. It is significant that of late some religious colonies, suffering from federal persecution, are considering emigration outside the United States. The Canaan and refuge of pilgrims is becoming their house of bondage.

The freedom of movement or emigration went hand in hand with an insistence on the validity and necessity of *local responsibility*. The two are inseparable. The very belief that a local group is *decisive* in its self-government and faith is important to the impulse to colonize and to experiment in government. Spanish and French colonies were weak in this motive, whereas the English colonies were either founded in terms of this faith *or* quickly developed it. Their ultimate claim to independence from parliamentary absolutism was a corollary to their emigration and their religious interpretation of that fact. The right to emigration meant cultural pluralism, *not* a national state. Modern interventionism is political, economic, and religious (but non-Christian and anti-Christian), and seeks a unitary state. The decline of the personal covenant of grace is the prelude to the decline of personal responsibility and the rise of statism.

Significantly, New England men remained zealous colonizers and settled the West. Indeed, American history can be viewed, as has been done by Chard Powers Smith in *Yankees and God*, as successive if waning revivals of Puritanism and the colonization by and conversion to Puritanism of the United States. (Smith dates the four Puritan revivals as follows: 1630-1660, 1700-1760, 1800-1860, 1900-1930, and the periods of decline: 1660-1700, 1760-1800, 1860-1900, 1930-1960.) Again, it can be viewed as "a contest for local autonomy as well as one for individual liberty."[4] Contempt for the feudal and pluralistic origins of the United States is the hallmark of statists, who call for the repression of "so-called grassroots democracy...to maintain a genuinely pluralistic society." Kariel's pluralism is the plethora of bureaucratic agencies![5] This is not the American heritage, but a modern revolution within the form, steadily seeking to destroy the American structure.

The New England men, in their westward migration, revealed a zeal to establish schools and colleges, institutions, associations, societies, and churches which very early made them leaders in the western states. As Tocqueville noted:

> We were assured in 1830, that thirty-six of the members of congress were born in the little state of Connecticut. The population of Connecticut, which constitutes only one forty-third part of that of the United States, thus furnished one eighth of the whole body of representatives. The state of Connecticut, however, only sends five delegates to congress; and the thirty-one others sit for the new western states.[6]

By 1860, a fourth of the population of Greater New England, i.e., the United States apart from the South and Southwest but inclusive of California, were "pure Yankees."[7]

This migration has sometimes been written off as purely economic, i.e., Yankees left the limited soil of New England and moved west to improve their lot. This opinion rests on the myth of the settlers' ability to live off the wilderness.[8] The romantic myth of bounteous nature holds that man had only to move into virgin territory to live richly and well. Actually, most Indians lived very meagerly, often on animals repulsive to white men, and sometimes starved. Indian bands within a tribe were often a handful, and each band required a wide expanse of territory and much migration in order to survive. Game was scarce in most areas, with some exceptions. Passenger pigeons were numerous but not even seasonal in their migration. Buffalo were important, but no tribe could live in their pathway. Deer were not plentiful, and rabbits were scarce, until the white man cleared the forests and created fields and grasslands. The abuse of some natural resources has been real, but the improvement of many even more notable. A near-continent barely supporting a few hundred thousand Indians now

---

[4.] Edward S. Corwin, *The "Higher Law" Background of American Constitutional Law* (Ithaca, N.Y.: Great Seal Books, Cornell, 1955), 81.
[5.] Henry S. Kariel, *The Decline of American Pluralism* (Stanford: Stanford University Press, 1961), 277.
[6.] Tocqueville, 321.
[7.] C. P. Smith, *Yankees and God* (New York: Hermitage House, 1954), 291, 303f., 499f.
[8.] See Jared Van Wagenen Jr., *The Golden Age of Homespun* (Ithaca, N.Y.: Cornell University Press, 1953), 90ff., for a critique of this myth.

supports an ever-increasing population. Grasslands grow richer grass, and most farmland has increased in fertility. The abuses have been real, but, statist propagandists and champions to the contrary, they are far from being the whole story. From the beginning, conservation *and* improvement have been practiced.

The romantic reading of history sees the Indian as a dedicated conservationist, forgetting that the Indian was heedless of the future and ready to set fires in order to drive game into his hungry hands. The statist reading of history bypasses the evidences of early American problems with the land in order to argue for state interference and control. As Malin has observed with reference to the grasslands, the most vivid description of a dust storm dates from 1830 in what is now north central Kansas when the Indians were in full possession. Dust storms are recorded for 1850-1900 in numerous accounts. It is the "most brazen falsehood...ever perpetrated upon a gullible public" to ascribe the dust storms of the 1930s to "The Plow that broke the Plains."[9]

The settler needed capital to migrate westward, supplies to keep alive a year or two, seeds, livestock, chickens, tools, and time both to clear the land and to improve it. His first harvests were often poor; the soil took time to develop, and often needed time, rotation, and enrichment. As he developed his land and its fertility, game flourished near it, and the game then began to attract Indians, who found deer, rabbits, and other such game closer to the white man than to the wilderness. But the settler could not depend on game for his table, and the vegetable bounty of the new country was even worse. Capital was thus a necessity, plus hard work, patience, courage, and faith.[10] Possessing these things, Americans moved to possess the land and, in Biblical terms, to inherit it. Immigrants from Europe in later years had to settle in similar fashion. Many a couple came to America in steerage, and then sank the bride's dowry in western land, and in supplies and equipment to develop that land. The settlers were families, and the wife and children hard-working members in a difficult venture. The lone frontiersman was a trapper, always well-stocked with provisions, or, after

---

[9]. James C. Malin, *The Grassland of North America: Prolegomena to its History* (Lawrence, Kansas: self-published, 1947), 138-140; and Malin, "The Grassland of North America: its Occupance and the Challenge of Continuous Reappraisals," Background Paper no. 19, prepared for the Wenner-Gren Foundation International Symposium, "Man's Role in Changing the Face of the Earth," (Princeton Inn, Princeton, N.J., June 16-22, 1955), 10. For Malin's account of the buffalo's effect on the plain, and other factors, see "Soil, Animal, and Plant Relations of the Grassland, Historically Reconsidered," *The Scientific Monthly*, April 1953, 207-220.

[10]. For evidence of this, as well as the group nature of settlements, see the Marquis de Chastellux, *Travels in North America in the Years 1780, 1781, and 1782*, vol. I (Chapel Hill: University of North Carolina Press, 1963), 79f. Two years were needed before self-support became possible for settlers. Moreover, this rapidity of settlement and self-support was possible because "in America a man is never alone, never an isolated being."

the Civil War, an ex-soldier, often Confederate, drifting into mining camps or towns dominated by large land and cattle companies, to act as a paid agent in warfare against the settler. The settlers were men with the frailties of men, often discouraged, ready to demand help as a right, ready to repent emotionally at revivals and camp meetings, but also men whose venture required capital, courage, patience, and faith. They were emigrants who had forsaken relatives and city to colonize, and the motive for colonization often appealed to was a religious sense of destiny: to possess a continent as the chosen people of God. In the Monroe Doctrine, this concept was applied to all the Americas, in that they were designated the area of *self-determination.* Henry Clay hoped that the United States would be "the head of the American system" as it spread through the Americas. It was hoped that, inspired by the example of the United States, Latin America would throw off its old world shackles and become with its "head" the truly *new* world. In this aspect, the Monroe Doctrine failed to attain its purpose.

Cotton Mather had believed that the New England colony would spark a blaze destined to re-illumine a darkened world with a new and greater Reformation. The survival and abuse of this hope has a long history in the United States. In its perversions, it has been a messianic faith. In its health, it has been the summons of the pilgrim Christian, bound for the Celestial City, to others to join him in that pilgrimage and the blessedness of a *Pilgrim's Progress.*

William Stoughton (1631-1701) expressed the sense of grace, and also of boldness in grace, which has characterized the American pilgrimage, in an election sermon of 1668:

> As for our advantages and privileges in a covenant state: here time and strength would fail to reckon up what we have enjoyed of this kind. If any people in the world have been lifted up to heaven as to advantages and privileges, we are the people. Name what you will under this head, and we have had it.... God sifted a whole nation that he might send choice grain over into this wilderness.

> Thus it hath been with us as to grounds of divine expectation. And therefore let us in the fear of God learn this great truth today, and receive the instruction thereof sealed up unto all our souls: That the great God hath taken up great expectations of us, and made great promises to Himself concerning us, and this hath been — and is — New England's day and season of probation.[11]

Timothy Dwight (1752-1817), in *The Conquest of Canaan* (1785), saw Americans as a new chosen people called by God to possess the land: "Arise, go over this Jordan, thou, and all this people, unto the land which I do give

---

[11.] Perry Miller, ed., *The American Puritans, Their Prose and Poetry* (Garden City, N.Y.: Doubleday Anchor, 1956), 115f.

them" (Joshua 1:2). This poem, immensely popular and influential in its day, underscores what many scholars tend to ignore: the colonials were not individualists seeking individual rights but a covenant people waging war against political and ecclesiastical absolutism in terms of a covenantal conception of law, liberty, and authority. They were emigrants and pilgrims, and America was their promised land. They looked confidently to the *future*, therefore. It is a significant and melancholy fact that their descendants now look nostalgically to the *past*, a perspective not calculated to ensure victory.

6

Liberty and Property

Biblical faith is land-oriented, and both the Old and New Testaments pronounce a beatitude upon the meek before God: they shall inherit the earth (Ps. 37:9; Matt. 5:5). In illustration, Naboth's religious loyalty to family and land is to be noted. Side by side with this land-based nature of biblical religion is also the pilgrimage note: the feast of tabernacles and the dwelling in booths as a reminder of Israel's wilderness journey emphasized their status as pilgrims towards tomorrow, God's great promise. Thus, family and land were rooted in yesterday, but, unlike other religions, Biblical faith was not past-bound: its central and tap root was in the future, and in terms of this man was and is a pilgrim, and he claims title to the land because all creation is to become his inheritance. His nature and destiny are of God; he holds the land from God and in terms of God's law and promises.

Some of the implications of this were noted by Bishop Sheen in his testimony before a congressional committee:

> There are several reasons why there is no place for God in communism. One is because of its concept of freedom. Suppose I correlate the problem of religion and the problem of freedom in answering your question, and let me begin with freedom and then go to religion.

> A man is free on the inside because he has a soul that he can call his own. Wherever you have the spirit you have freedom. A pencil has no freedom, ice has no freedom to be warm, fire has no freedom to be cold. You begin to have freedom only when you have something immaterial or spiritual.

49

Now, freedom must have some external guaranty of itself. The external guaranty of human freedom is property. A man is free on the inside because he can call his soul his own; he is free on the outside because he can call something he has his own. Therefore private property is the economic guaranty of human freedom.

Suppose now you concoct a system in which you want to possess man totally. On what conditions can you erect a totalitarian system so that man belongs to you completely? One, you have got to deny spirit; two, you have got to deny property.

That is why the existence of God and private property are both denied simultaneously by communism. If a man has no soul, he cannot allege that he has any relationships with anyone outside of the state. If he has no property, he is dependent upon the state even for his physical existence. Therefore the denial of God and the denial of freedom are both conditions of slavery.[1]

We have seen that the colonial concepts of government and of liberty were developments of feudalism, again a land-based system. It is not surprising that the watchword of the Sons of Liberty was "Liberty and Property."[2] The two were common causes in English history. The long struggle for protection of *property and person* from the absolute claims of the king had a mixed victory in 1688. Trial by jury and other liberties were gained, but also parliamentary absolutism. The legal protection of property had a long legal history in England. Thus, the law requiring the death penalty for every man, woman, or child who stole property to the value of five shillings had a 200 year history.[3] The unfairness of the penalty has been recognized, but the law, commonly ascribed to the eighteenth century only, also made clear the strong sense of property in England.

The significance of property was discussed in Cromwell's army during the Putney Debates in 1647. Ireton spoke of "the most original, the most fundamental civil constitution of this kingdom, and which is, above all, that constitution by which I have any property."[4] Ireton declared further, in a discussion of suffrage (a forty shilling freehold gave suffrage, whereas a hundred pounds a year leasehold did not):

> The people's falling into a government is for the preservation of property.... What weight there lies in this: since there is a falling into government and government is to preserve property, therefore this cannot be against property. The objection does not lie in that, the

[1] *The Ideological Fallacies of Communism*, Staff Consultations with Rabbi S. Andhil Finebert, Bishop Fulton J. Sheen, Dr. Daniel A. Poling. September 4, 25, October 18, 1957. Committee on Un-American Activities, House of Representatives, 85th Congress (Washington, D.C.: G.P.O., 1958), 11.
[2] R. V. Coleman, *Liberty and Property* (New York: Scribner, 1951), 530f.
[3] Francis H. Heller, *The Sixth Amendment to the Constitution of the United States, A Study in Constitutional Development* (Lawrence, Kansas: University of Kansas Press, 1951), 13.
[4] A. S. P. Woodhouse, ed., *Puritanism and Liberty* (London: Dent, 1938), 60.

making of the representation more equal, but the introducing of men into an equality of interest in this government, who have no property in this kingdom, or who have no local permanent interest in it.... I do not mean that I would have it restrained to that proportion (that now obtains), but to restrain it still to men who have a local, a permanent interest in the kingdom, who have such an interest that they may live upon it as freemen, and who have such an interest as is fixed upon a place, and is not the same equally everywhere.[5]

Ireton argued against soldiers who asked why they should have no vote, having fought for their country. Ireton did not place a class restriction upon voting: a wealthy man without locally owned property, holding only leases, had no right to vote. For Ireton, as for untold others, property and liberty were concepts related to *localism*. Property and power had to be local, and trustworthy wealth was landed wealth. Liberty rested on this relationship. Responsibility and liberty began at home.

This faith crossed the Atlantic with the colonists and flourished there. The *county*, today the neglected unit, became under the developing colonial and early federal governments the basic American unit of government. For some generations in United States history, the primary importance of the local and county units governed political life. Presidential elections could not compete in importance with state politics, and local and sectional interests governed federal elections, so that Federalist, Republican, American Democratic, and Whig elections were often heavily influenced by non-federal factors. After Washington, no president at least through Lincoln, could be said to be a nationally popular figure, because the federal government did not sufficiently dominate or control the republic to give such stature to a president. It is a mistake to read present evaluations, and the heat of party newspapers of the times, into the popular mind of that day. The triumph of Jefferson, thus, was not a popular movement (John Adams may indeed have had a slightly stronger following), but rather the result of political organization and the able manipulation of local and sectional interests. The Jeffersonians represented an intelligent and able political group rather than a popular movement.[6] The strategic importance of localism, politically and economically, is by no means gone. Land and personal property taxes, as well as basic criminal law, are still in county hands, making it the main bulwark against the power of Washington, D.C., and the states. Any restoration or essential development of American constitutionalism must involve a revival of localism. It is significant that the

---

[5.] *Ibid.*, 62.
[6.] See Stephen C. Kurtz, *The Presidency of John Adams, The Collapse of Federalism, 1795-1800* (Philadelphia: University of Pennsylvania Press, 1957), 91., 137f; and Noble E. Cunningham Jr., *The Jeffersonian Republicans, The Formation of Party Organization, 1789-1801* (Chapel Hill: University of North Carolina Press, 1957).

mounting statist movement has launched an attack on the integrity of county power.

Basic to any renewal of localism are three things:

1) The religious recognition that the basic government is self-government. There is no freedom for men who will not be responsible. This is, of course, the personal covenant of grace, the responsibility of the Christian man before God.

2) Free and responsible men see as their most important obligations those nearest home. If they fail in the immediate responsibility, they cannot be capable of meeting a distant one. Hence, with responsibility, there is major concern with local government, be it personal, family, societal, township, or county. The old Bostonian attitude that an office in Boston or Harvard is more important than an office in Washington is a faint trace of this belief.

3) A restoration of religious faith in the significance of real property, and the relationship of ownership and power, is necessary. It should be noted that much of what is written off as land speculation among the founding fathers involved also a religious sense concerning land, and an association of land with true wealth. As has been noted of George Washington:

> A typical instance of his craving for land is an episode that occurred after the war. While traveling in upstate New York with Governor George Clinton he saw a beautiful woodland, and though he had no cash, was already burdened with debts for land purchases, and was unlikely ever to see that land again, he arranged to borrow $6,000 from Clinton and bought it on the spot.[7]

During the Constitutional Convention and after, many spoke of the necessity of restricting suffrage to men of property. On this basis, Marxists have attacked the Constitution and the founding fathers as men of a narrow and class perspective. Consequently, some have portrayed subsequent history as the progressive liberalization of ostensibly harsh laws which kept most people from voting.

In answer to these positions, it must be observed, first of all, that the fear of the property-less man's vote was often very different from what the modern radical or leftist assumes it to have been. The full statement of Madison during the Convention debates needs to be examined:

> Mr. MADISON. The right of suffrage is certainly one of the fundamental articles of republican Government, and ought not to be left to be regulated by the Legislature. A gradual abridgment of this right has been the mode in which Aristocracies have been built on the ruins of popular forms. Whether the Constitutional qualification

---

[7.] Forrest McDonald, *We the People, The Economic Origins of the Constitution*, (Chicago: University of Chicago Press, 1958), 70f.

ought to be a freehold, would with him depend much on the probable reception such a change would meet with in States where the right was now exercised by every description of people. In several of the States a freehold was now the qualification. Viewing the subject in its merits alone, the freeholders of the Country would be the safest depositories of Republican liberty. In future times a great majority of the people will not only be without landed, but any other sort of, property. These will either combine under the influence of their common situation; in which case, the rights of property & the public liberty, will not be secure in their hands: or which is more probable, they will become the tools of opulence & ambition, in which case there will be equal danger on another side. The example of England has been misconceived (by Col. Mason). A very small proportion of the Representatives are there chosen by freeholders. The greatest part are chosen by the Cities & boroughs, in many of which the qualification of suffrage is as low as it is in any one of the U.S. and it was in the boroughs & Cities rather than the Counties, that bribery most prevailed, & the influence of the Crown on elections was most dangerously exerted.[8]

Madison recognized the possibility that property-less men would unite against the rest of society, but he did not consider it likely. Rather, he felt it "more probable" that such men would "become the tools of opulence and ambition," so that a new "aristocracy" would rule, using the masses as its tools. The result would be an oligarchy ruling in the name of the people. Gouverneur Morris, in the same debate, affirmed a similar position:

It was the thing, not the name, to which he was opposed, and one of his principal objections to the Constitution as it is now before us, is that it threatens this Country with an Aristocracy. The aristocracy will grow out of the House of Representatives. Give the votes to people who have no property, and they will sell them to the rich who will be able to buy them. We should not confine our attention to the present moment. The time is not distant when this Country will abound with mechanics & manufacturers who will receive their bread from their employers. Will such men be the secure & faithful Guardians of liberty? Will they be the impregnable barrier ag'st aristocracy? — He is as little duped by the association of the words "taxation & Representation." The man who does not give his vote freely is not represented. It is the man who dictates the vote. Children do not vote. Why? because they want prudence, because they have no will of their own. The ignorant & the dependent can be as little trusted with the public interest. He did not conceive the difficulty of defining "freeholders" to be insuperable. Still less that the restriction could be unpopular. 9/10 of the people are at present freeholders and these will certainly be pleased with it. As to Merch'ts & c. if they have wealth & value the right they can acquire it. If not they don't deserve it.[9]

[8.] Charles C. Tansill, ed.,*Documents Illustrative of the Formation of the Union of the American States*, 69th Congress, 1st Session, House Document No. 398 (Washington D.C.: GPO, 1927), 489f.

[9.] *Ibid.*, 488f.

Notice again that Morris feared that property-less men, if granted the suffrage, would usher in the rule of an aristocracy! The poor would be controlled in their voting by the great and the rich, their masters.[10]

That Madison and Morris were right, recent events have substantiated. The presidency, if not held by men of great wealth, is increasingly controlled by them, and the cabinet, especially under Kennedy, has represented an amazing concentration of wealth. Through the manipulation of labor votes, powerful financial and industrial interests, the modern oligarchy, are the effectual power in Washington, which has become hostile to a free-market economy but favorable to oligarchy.

The other members of the Constitutional Convention did not foresee the future problems feared by Morris and Madison. James Wilson called attention to the widespread suffrage (nine-tenths according to Morris' statement) in the states; to restrict suffrage by stricter federal regulations would lead to problems. Mason commented, "Eight or nine States have extended the right of suffrage beyond the freeholders, what will the people there say, if they should be disfranchised." Dickinson pointed out that, since "the great mass of our Citizens is composed at this time of freeholders," no departure from tradition would be involved, and no "innovation." Rutledge feared that a constitutional restriction would be a divisive measure.[11] But Morris insisted, "unless you establish a qualification of Property, we shall have an aristocracy."[12] This then was the fear. Those disagreeing with Madison and Morris did not favor an aristocracy or oligarchy: they simply did not foresee the danger, and, since almost all Americans were *already* freeholders, the question was to them an academic one.

Second, as has already been indicated, property-less men were, in all the states, at that time very few, and in some areas a rarity. A detailed study of suffrage in Massachusetts has confirmed this. Virtually all Massachusetts men could meet the property requirement. An aristocracy and a lower class were scarcely in existence. "In Massachusetts, therefore, we find one of the unique 'revolutions' in world history—a revolution to preserve a social order rather than to change it."[13] As Boorstin has remarked:

> The most obvious peculiarity of our American Revolution is that, in the modern European sense of the word, it was hardly a revolution at all. The Daughters of the American Revolution, who have been

---

[10]. Chilton Williamson, *American Suffrage from Property to Democracy, 1760-1860* (Princeton, N.J.: Princeton University Press, 1960), 126.
[11]. *Documents Illustrative of the Formation of the Union,* 487-491.
[12]. *Ibid.,* 874.
[13]. Robert E. Brown, *Middle-Class Democracy and the Revolution in Massachusetts, 1691-1780* (Ithaca, N.Y.: Cornell University Press, 1955), 401. See in this connection also Charles S. Grant, *Democracy in the Connecticut Frontier Town of Kent* (New York: Columbia University Press, 1961).

understandably sensitive on this subject, have always insisted in their literature that the American Revolution was no revolution but merely a colonial rebellion. The more I have looked into the subject, the more convinced I have become of the wisdom of their naivete.[14]

Some years later, Tocqueville reported, with reference to property and suffrage:

> In America those complaints against property in general, which are so frequent in Europe, are never heard, because in America there are no paupers; and as every one has property of his own to defend, every one recognizes the principle upon which he holds it.[15]

> In the United States, except slaves, servants, and paupers in the receipt of relief from the townships, there is no class of persons who do not exercise the elective franchise, and who do not contribute indirectly to make the laws.[16]

The people of the United States were then, and for some time thereafter, freeholders, and the correlation of property and power was taken for granted.

Third, as Brown's study among others indicates, the property requirement was higher in local than in state elections, with none on the federal level. Neither the Revolution nor the federal union led to a liberalization of the property requirement. The Northwest Ordinance, reenacted by the new government, established thus before and after the Constitution a fifty-acre freehold qualification. North Carolina alone had an equally high requirement.[17]

Fourth, the basic premise of colonial legislation on suffrage had been the necessity of demonstrable Christian character:

> It is obvious from this description of colonial suffrage legislation that it was designed to confine the vote to desirable elements of the population. It was drafted in the conviction that efficiency, honesty, and harmony in government rested, in the last analysis, upon a salutary degree of homogeneity of interests, opinions, and fundamental loyalties—religious, ethnic, and class. Confining the vote in colony elections to those who were free, white, twenty-one, native-born Protestant males who were the owners of property, especially real property, appeared to be the best guarantee of the stability of the commonwealth. The drafters of colonial suffrage legislation, to whatever extent they attempted to formulate ideas, seem to have thought that undue disparities of interest, opinion, and loyalty among electors would weaken and distract government. It is in the

---

14. Daniel J. Boorstin, *The Genius of American Politics* (Chicago: The University of Chicago Press, 1953), 68f.
15. Alexis de Tocqueville, *Democracy in America*, vol. I (New York: Langley, 1841), 266.
16. *Ibid.*, 268.
17. Williamson, 117.

light of their principles, rather than those of the present times, that the suffrage laws of colonial times can be understood.[18]

It should be noted that, by 1776 the colonies had a greater degree of homogeneity than ever before. The South at this time, as well as Pennsylvania and other areas, had been, first, subject to great waves of immigration, and, second, to an extensive religious revival. Englishmen and Scotch, Scotch-Irish, and German yeomanry had entered Southern states in such numbers that the old settlers were far outnumbered. Thus, during the Revolutionary period, the white population of North Carolina was tripled, and that of South Carolina quadrupled.[19] The period from 1760 on, seen by Chard Powers Smith and others as a time of religious decline from the perspective of New England, was elsewhere, and especially in the South, a time of religious revival. The intensely held faith of these people was usually Reformed, and thus not unlike New England Puritanism in many respects. It could be reasonably argued that, for some time to come, the mainspring of American Puritanism moved southward, and that there the conception of the holy commonwealth prospered. Unitarianism subsequently developed in New England even as trinitarian orthodoxy triumphed elsewhere. A Roman Catholic scholar, commenting on the Calvinist Jedidiah Morse and his battle against the Illuminati in New England, has observed:

> The Illuminati, *qua* organization, did not have the effect on American politics attributed to it, *qua* crystallization of the "Zeitgeist," they changed the trend of continental Freemasonry, animated the French Revolution, and via France, came to America, where they changed theocratic New England into a secularist country, almost anti-clerical in its public policy.[20]

This decline, however, came later. At the time of the Revolution and much later, New England and the rest of the country shared a common faith and perspective.

Fifth, irrespective of the issue of suffrage, property was seen as the necessary basis of the economic aspect of society. Jefferson's agrarianism was in part based on his strong adherence to a freehold society rather than a property-less and money-based urban society. It was recognized that *property meant inequality*, since property and the freedom to acquire property leads to diverse conditions for men. But, it was held, *liberty and*

---

18. *Ibid.*, 19. The perspective of Williamson's study is different from that of this writer.

19. Henry Savage Jr., *Seeds of Time, The Background of Southern Thinking* (New York: Holt, Rinehart and Winston, 1959), 32.

20. Arthur Preuss, *A Dictionary of Secret and Other Societies* (St. Louis, Mo.: Herder, 1924), 77f. See with reference to Jedidiah Morse and the New England scene, Vernon Stauffer, *New England and the Bavarian Illuminati*; for George Washington's comment on Morse's crusade against the Illuminati, see 342f. See also Jedidiah Morse, Sermon, *The Day of the National Fast*, April 25, 1799 (Charleston, 1799).

equality could not coexist: the right to liberty ensured inequality, in that under freedom some men would excel. Both Federalists and Republicans were in agreement on this point later, and, earlier, at the Constitutional Convention, June 26, 1787, Hamilton agreed with Madison's comments on this question, declaring:

> It was certainly true: that nothing like an equality of property existed: that an inequality would exist as long as liberty existed, and that it would unavoidably result from that very liberty itself.[21]

Sixth, the *extension* of suffrage rights did not coincide with the rise of democratic thought in the modern sense, nor with Jacksonianism. The "Farmers' Age" led to something very much like the agrarian republic Jefferson desired and was thus a time of property ownership, i.e., real property. Freehold tenure lagged in New York but prevailed generally elsewhere.[22] The old freehold requirements were easily met, and a fifty-acre requirement was no problem. The relaxation of this and similar requirements came, first, out of a sense of confidence in the freehold basis of the United States, and, second, from a belief in the limitation of powers and a distrust of privilege. Thus, James Fenimore Cooper, by no means a champion of the "left" of his day, declared in 1838:

> When property rules, it rules alone; but when the poor are admitted to have a voice in government, the rich are never excluded. Such is the nature of man, that all exclusive power is uniformly directed to exclusive purposes. Property always carries with it a portion of political influence, and it is unwise, and even dangerous, to strengthen this influence by adding to it constitutional privileges; the result always being to make the strong stronger, and the weak weaker.[23]

Cooper's premise was a distrust of any government which represented a particular group, rich or poor, propertied or non-propertied, on a national level. On the local level, Cooper believed in a more restricted suffrage in terms of local interests. This was, of course, the basic pattern in many areas. It represented a faith in the centrality of the local unit. "Universal suffrage," Cooper held, was a foolish term, in that, first, women were excluded, as well as males under age. Furthermore, paupers, criminals, vagabonds, and aliens were also excluded. Moreover,

> The governments of towns and villages, for instance, are almost entirely directed to the regulation of property, and to the control of local interests. In such governments universal suffrage is clearly misplaced, for several grave and obvious reasons, a few of which shall

---

[21.] *Documents Illustrative of the Formation of the Union*, 282. These are, of course, Madison's summary reports of the Debates.
[22.] See Paul W. Gates, *The Farmer's Age: Agriculture 1815-1860*, vol. III, *The Economic History of the United States* (New York: Holt, Rinehart and Winston, 1960), 36ff.
[23.] James Fenimore Cooper, *The American Democrat* (New York: Vintage Books, 1956), 136.

be mentioned. The laws which control the great and predominant interests, or those which give a complexion to society, emanate from the states, which may well enough possess a wide political base. But towns and Villages regulating property chiefly, there is a peculiar propriety in excluding those from the suffrage who have no immediate local interests in them.[24]

The principle here is obvious: the basis of county government is its power to tax property, real property in particular. To break down this liberty of the local property owner to govern himself by introducing the control of property-less voters over his property is to *destroy* the foundations of society in the American and in the Christian sense. In some states, to this day, the right in counties to vote on tax and bond issues is limited to property owners. On state and federal levels, since the basis of taxation and government is citizenship or residence, not property, it was deemed only just that each citizen of good character, meeting the various requirements of mature and responsible citizenship, should have the right of suffrage. The relationship of *property and liberty* is thus critical at the county level, and the centrality of county politics in early American history is unduly neglected. Its neglect has substantially contributed to the decline of the American system.

Attempts to eliminate the county as obsolete and redundant are thus attempts to destroy America as a republic and as a federal system. Indirect attempts have also been prevalent. Two may be cited in passing. First, federal subsidies have undermined the independence and authority of county governments. Second, state-sponsored property tax exemptions for war veterans have produced two generations of men who are unmindful of the burdens placed upon property and the erosion of property rights.

The continuing vitality of the county, however, must not be discounted. Neglected by voters who are ignorant of its importance, it is indeed often heavily weighted with incompetent and dishonest men. Nonetheless, it is an area where thousands of dedicated men are waging a major battle for the American system.

Significantly, too, the county is the last area where religious tests for teachers and civil officers have maintained their vitality, whether openly or tacitly. Suffrage restrictions also have had their major stand, both for good and evil, primarily in terms of county politics.

Finally, the stress on property was secondarily economic and primarily ethical. The man of property had at least the character to provide for

---

[24.] *Ibid.* Karl Marx observed, in stated agreement with Alexander Hamilton, that "man proclaims politically that private property is abolished as soon as he abolishes the property qualification for the vote... Is not private property as an idea abolished when the non-owner becomes legislator for the owner? The property qualification for the vote *is* the ultimate political form of the recognition of private property." Karl Marx, *A World Without Jews* (New York: Philosophical Library, 1960), 11.

himself and his family and to develop an inheritance. Madison was opposed to a *landed* qualification for office in that "Landed possessions were no certain evidence of real wealth. Many enjoyed them to a great extent who were more in debt than they were worth....Some other criterion than the mere possession of land should be devised" as a property test.[25] Debt and irresponsible management did not meet the moral test Madison had in mind with respect to property, and debt made ownership null.

The principle, as Felix Morley has observed in an unpublished lecture, was *qualitative, not quantitative*. The New England "selectmen" were more than elected men: they were intended to be *select* men. The basis of suffrage and representation was responsible character. Hence, no recipient of government subsidy or charity could vote. The original idea of the poll tax was to establish responsibility: the responsible taxpayer was made the voter.[26]

The first attack on local responsibility came early in the nineteenth century with the exploitation of the possibilities of a clause in the Constitution, Article II, Section I, with reference to the electoral college:

> Each state shall appoint, in such manner as the Legislature thereof may direct, a number of Electors, equal to the whole number of Senators and Representatives to which the state may be entitled in the Congress; but no Senator or Representative, or person holding an office of trust or profit under the United States, shall be appointed an Elector.

While not dictating to the states, the Constitution, by paralleling the electors to the congressional structure, at least suggested a similar means of election to the states. At first, some states chose their electors by congressional districts, with two at large to represent the senators, or by legislative act, or other means. Gradually, state politicians realized the power inherent in control of the total electors by means of a state-wide vote for the entire list. The state majority thereby overruled the congressional district and gave the electoral vote to the urban political boss. "In 1836, the general ticket system was used in every State but South Carolina, which continued to elect by legislature through 1860." Three exceptions have occurred since then. "They were Florida in 1868 and Colorado in 1876, in which the elections were by the legislature, and Michigan in 1892 when the district system with two electors at-large was used." The real problem then with the electoral college is not in its structure. "The real culprit is the use of the general ticket by every State." Legislation to correct this situation has been proposed by Karl E. Mundt, U.S. Senator, South Dakota.[27] A basic premise of this proposal is the restoration of control to the congressional

---

25. *Documents Illustrative of the Formation of the Union*, 461f.
26. Felix Morley, "Institutional Decay," 28 August 1962, St. Mary's College, California.

district in the election of president. It is in spirit a part of the long-standing insistence on local responsibility which is basic to the American belief in liberty and property. [28]

---

27. Karl E. Mundt, "Is Your Presidential Vote Worth MORE or LESS Than Your Neighbor's?," *Dawn*, 7, no. 7, September, 1962, 4, 6.

28. For an excellent essay on the importance and significance of local history, see James C. Malin, "On the Nature of Local History," *Wisconsin Magazine of History*, Summer 1957, 227-230.

7

Equality

Attempts are sometimes made to force the New Deal ideas of equality onto the American Revolution or Rebellion, or to see U. S. history as a long struggle to realize what the twentieth century liberal believes. The result has been historical confusion.[1]

It should be noted, however, that attempts to read the Revolution as egalitarianism were first made by enemies of the Continental Congress who sought to tar the Colonial cause with the brush of radicalism. Thus, one Tory poem described the rival suitors of the maiden liberty with such ridicule:

> After John Presbyter
> Will Democrat came next,
> Who swore all men were even
> And seemed to be quite vext,
> That there's a king in heaven.
> Will curst the hilly country 'round
> Because it made unequal ground.[2]

Since the colonials were and are also accused of being capitalistic smugglers, with a little more truth, we can discount this Tory humor.

Discussions of equality are usually characterized by a fuzziness of language, since the term is usually a political slogan and as such is evasive of

---

[1] See J. Franklin Jameson, *The American Revolution Considered As a Social Movement* (New York: Peter Smith, 1950).

[2] Charles Halstead Van Tyne, *The Loyalists in the American Revolution* (New York: Macmillan, 1902), 105.

meaning. A few of the many concepts of equality can be cited as a step towards clarification of the issue.

First, the *rational* ideal or concept of equality has been influential in modern history. In this faith, an abstract concept of man is held to be true irrespective of any and all circumstances concerning the individual. This is essentially a religious faith, but, having been affirmed by humanists who pride themselves on their rationalism, the name can be used even as its irrationality is noted. In terms of the rationalism of this school, man is logically a certain kind of being possessed of certain natural attributes, of which equality is central. This is the *reality* concerning man; all factors pointing to another condition are ruled to be historical, cultural, or environmental *accidents*. Hence the accidents must be eliminated and the reality allowed to flourish.

Second, the *scientific* doctrine of equality, while in essence the same as the rational, saw its proof not in reason but in science. Thus, behaviorism assumed all human materials to be equal, and Watson believed every man to be capable of all things *if* totally conditioned by behavioristic science. So-called scientific socialism, similarly a latter-day "rationalism" or religion of man, has often used this doctrine.

Third, there is the doctrine of *empirical* equality, which holds that equal conditions or success imply equal men. Thus, the American Indian has often assumed the equality of white men, as equally successful, and assumed his superiority to the Negro ("We fought, but they became slaves") because of unequal factors. Socially, this doctrine is assumed as people strive to attain a certain degree of wealth and circumstance and assume that they are thereby entitled to move in a particular strata of society as equals. This concept thus has reference to external factors and conditions.

Fourth, the concept of *political* equality in the sense of equal suffrage is affirmed. All men are, in terms of certain principles, i.e., age and character requirements, eligible to vote. In California, various extensions of this concept have been proposed: dropping the reading requirement for suffrage, and the automatic restoration of suffrage to ex-convicts. Elsewhere, a lowering of the age requirement has been suggested. The 19th Amendment (1920) was in part an expression of this concept.

Fifth, *sexual* equality, also expressed in the feminist movement, is an assertion that the differences between men and women are accidents (in the philosophical sense), their *reality* being a common and an equal condition. This concept is again a by-product of "rationalism" and humanism and presupposes that differences are invidious and uniformity ideal.

Civil equality is a sixth definition of this concept. In this doctrine, all men, irrespective of political and other conditions, are equal before the law, and equally eligible for taxation, jury duty, military service, and other responsibilities of citizenship. This again was not a characteristic of the federal union in its origins. Slaves were the conspicuous exception. Taxation rested on property on the county level, not on all persons. Not all served or do serve on juries or in the armed forces, although totalitarian regimes strive for this goal in their total-war concept. Emigration is restricted; certain political tenets are forbidden and have no status before the law as parties; the law establishes and enforces certain differences. To speak of justice is not thereby to speak of equality.

Seventh, *equality* of condition, or total communism, is also held. Equality of condition, as Cooper noted, means total communism and anarchy, since government institutes a fundamental inequality as soon as some are given a position of authority, however limited, over others.

Numerous other definitions of equality could be cited. An eighth will suffice, since it is, in terms of modern thought, central. *Equality is a mathematical term*, and it represents an abstraction and is an important concept in dealing with abstractions. But it cannot be applied to the concreteness, wholeness, and diversity of life without radical distortions. The growth of the political use of this mathematical concept has contributed to political and social confusion in the modern era. Equal and unequal are valid terms in their place, but untenable concepts elsewhere. It was the French Revolution which made the idea of equality a major political factor, although its previous history cannot be underrated.

The colonials made use of the word, and it appears in the Declaration of Independence. But in what sense? Its first and paramount use therein is usually bypassed: the Declaration affirmed it now to be "necessary" for the United States "to assume among the Powers of the earth, the separate and equal station to which the Laws of Nature and of Nature's God entitles them." Rosenstock-Huessy has noted the meaning:

> The colonies desired equality with the motherland. The French word *e'galite'*, the rallying-cry of 1789, meant equality within one country. Equal the citizen should be, regardless of vocation or profession. The American word equality, in 1776, was much less individualistic. The whole body politic of the colonies was jealous of the pretensions of the body politic at home. The colony of Massachusetts called itself the Commonwealth of Massachusetts; the name United States recalled the United Kingdom. George Washington could be compared with the noblest and best type of English gentleman. The American state papers were written in a peerless style of parliamentary English. The content of the American Revolution was no novelty, no new discovery of the nature of man; it was, first of all, an assertion of the *equal* right of the pioneers to have their English way in the new world.
>
> The inferiority complex of many educated Americans has its counterpart in the epoch of independence; the unquestioned leadership of Europe is to give way to an equality of the new States

with the old Monarchies, or, as the Preamble of the Declaration says, "an equal station among the Powers of the Earth." This Equality of 1776 still belongs to the Anglo-Saxon world of values; whereas the Egalite of 1789 was a radical outcry of men's individual nature.

The first version of Equality had been: We, the colonies, are the peers of the motherland. The second version, eleven years later, took cognizance of the tremendous universality of every word that is uttered by human faith.[3]

As Malin has also observed, "Independence meant, not isolation, but 'equality' of independent sovereign action within the family of nations."[4]

The second use of "equal" in the Declaration had reference to men: "We hold these truths to be self-evident, that all men are created equal, that they are endowed by their Creator with certain unalienable rights, that among these are Life, Liberty and the pursuit of Happiness."[5] This revised draft, submitted by Jefferson on June 28, 1776, was based on the first Article of the Virginia Bill of Rights, written by George Mason and passed by the Virginia legislature June 12, 1776. Their common meaning will better appear when both are viewed. The Virginia Bill of Rights reads thus:

> A declaration of rights made by the representatives of the good people of Virginia, assembled in full and free convention; which rights do pertain to them and their posterity, as the basis and foundation of government.
>
> SECTION 1. That all men are by nature equally free and independent, and have certain inherent rights, of which, when they enter into a state of society, they cannot, by any compact, deprive or divest their posterity; namely, the enjoyment of life and liberty, with the means of acquiring and possessing property, and pursuing and obtaining happiness and safety.

[3.] Eugen Rosenstock-Huessy, *Out of Revolution* (New York: William Morrow, 1938), 648.

[4.] James C. Malin, *The Contriving Brain and the Skillful Hand, Something About History and Philosophy of History* (Lawrence, Ks,: self-published, 1955), 11.

[5.] Jefferson's personal opinions on equality hardly conform to the modern liberal's picture of him. Greatly influenced by Plato's *Republic*, Jefferson believed in the special privileges of the elite like himself, including harems so that they might more extensively transmit their superior qualities. See Lester J. Cappon, *The Adams-Jefferson Letters, The Complete Correspondence Between Thomas Jefferson and Abigail and John Adams*, vol. II (Chapel Hill: University of North Carolina Press, 1959), 387ff.; Jefferson referred to the workers "of the cities of Europe" as "Canaille," 391. President Andrew Johnson much later observed, "The man who deliberately and boldly asserts that Thomas Jefferson, when he penned the sentiment that all men were created equal, had the negro in his mind, is either an *idiot* or a *knave*," *The Old Guard*, 3, no. XI (November, 1865), 528. It should also be noted that Senator Robert Toombs of Georgia, January 7, 1861, in the Senate, two weeks after the South Carolina Ordinance, concluded his address by affirming, in terms of contemporary usage, "Liberty and Equality" to be the Southern cause: "You present us war. We accept it; and, inscribing upon our banners the glorious words, 'Liberty and Equality,' we will trust to the blood of the brave, and the God of Battles, for security and tranquility." Alexander H. Stephens, *A Constitutional View of the Late War Between the States*, vol. II (Philadelphia: National, 1870), 125f.

As the Bill of Rights continues to specify its legal doctrine, it becomes apparent that this is a document by Virginians for Virginians: it is "by the representatives of the good people of Virginia...which rights do pertain to them and their posterity." It may perhaps be disillusioning to recognize this limitation, but it is the historical reality. And the Declaration likewise was governed by a limitation: the equal men were the free-born colonial men. They were distressed by the entangling legal fact of slavery, and almost half of the men favored its abolition legally, and over half desired it but, in the Constitutional Convention, they favored unity over a forced decision, believing that slavery would soon disappear. But, at the most, their opinion was that the Negro was equal to other Negroes and did not have a place in American society.

It is easy to read into the past, where we see *actions* or *words* comparable to those now held desirable, a similar *motive* or *rationale*. Thus, we find very early a demand for abolition, as witness Rev. Samuel Hopkins and others. The existence of slavery in the Colonies was quickly regretted, and steps were taken to end it. But the legislation towards that purpose is revealing. Thus, in 1692, in Virginia, legal provision was made for the manumission of Negro slaves, but on the condition that the Negro be transported out of the country within six months.[6] This legislation is indicative of the general temper: slavery was regarded as an evil, even by slaveholders, and its existence as inevitably doomed. For most Americans, the abolition of slavery meant also the *abolition of the Negro* from American life. Liberia was founded in terms of this hope, which was not peripheral but basic to much American thinking. The American Colonization Society, founded in 1817, was organized to resettle Negroes in Africa, a hope advocated by Washington, Jefferson, Madison, Monroe, John Marshall, Andrew Jackson, Henry Clay, Daniel Webster, Abraham Lincoln, and others. Lincoln, in his debates with Douglas, made it clear that he felt that the Negro was inferior and separation was necessary. Indeed, many statements made by these men as commonplaces of their day would today tar a man with the charge of racism.[7]

The American Colonization Society was very quickly approved by men in high places and by the Georgia and Tennessee legislatures. Chapters of the Society were established throughout the South, especially in Virginia,

---

6. Richard Hildreth, *The History of the United States*, vol. II, rev. ed. (New York: Harper, 1882), 179.
7. For Lincoln's views, see Paul M. Angle, ed., *Created Equal? The Complete Lincoln-Douglas Debates of 1858* (Chicago: University of Chicago Press, 1958), 117, 235f., 267f., 326-328. Lincoln did hold that the "created equal" phrase of the Declaration of Independence did apply to the Negroes in their right to "life, liberty, and the pursuit of happiness," 82. David Donald, *Lincoln Reconsidered* (New York: Vintage, 1961), 135f., while recognizing Lincoln's words on the Negro, holds without evidence the theory that these were "official" expressions and that Lincoln was "color-blind."

Kentucky, and Tennessee. "Of the hundred and thirty antislavery societies organized in the country, more than two thirds were in the South."[8] However, when, in 1824, the Ohio legislature, joined by eight other states, asked Congress to consider general and gradual emancipation and colonization at federal expense, it was ignored by the South. Nonetheless, in 1832, the Virginia legislature came very close to adopting abolition. The political overtones of the situation were clearly apparent in the fact that South Carolina took the lead in secession on Lincoln's election. South Carolina had suffered heavy losses economically through both slavery and cotton and had declined in eminence both sectionally and federally, and its bitterness was political. This political bitterness was reciprocated by many Northerners who had no desire for abolition and less desire for any common life with the Negro.

Thus, while there was much feeling on Christian or humanitarian grounds against slavery, there was, prior to the Civil War, equally strong and stronger feelings against the Negro as a part of the republic. Tocqueville noted this, and the fact that free Negroes in the north dared not presume to be equal with the whites:

> On the contrary, the prejudice of the race appears to be stronger in the states which have abolished slavery, than in those where it still exists; and nowhere is it so intolerant as in those states where servitude has never been known.

> Not only is slavery prohibited in Ohio, but no free negroes are allowed to enter the territory of that state, or to hold property in it.[9]

Malin's studies have confirmed this fact:

> In the free states, with few exceptions, the free negro did not exercise the civil rights of free white men, and in the states bordering the Ohio river on the north, free negroes were not wanted. The original institutions of those states had been formed by the small farmer element from the slave states who were predominantly antislavery and antinegro.[10]

Tocqueville had commented on the absence of a lower class and an aristocracy. In spite of this, Cooper felt there was more inequality in the United States than elsewhere.[11] In the sense that there was a wide variety

---

[8.] Henry Savage Jr., *Seed of Time, The Background of Southern Thinking* (New York: Holt, Rinehart and Winston, 1959), 62. Colonization ideas were reflected in Mary Griffith's *Three Hundred Years Hence,* published in Philadelphia in 1836. Mrs. Griffith "foresaw" all Negroes transplanted to Liberia (Philadelphia: Prime Press, 1950), 126.

[9.] Alexis de Tocqueville, *Democracy in America,* vol. I (New York: Langley, 1841), 389, 392.

[10.] James C. Malin, *The Nebraska Question 1852-1854* (Lawrence, Ks.: self-published, 1953), 393.

[11.] James Fennimore Cooper, *The American Democrat* (New York: Vintage Books, 1956), 43ff.

of differences, cultural and societal, this was in a sense true. Cooper rightfully denied the validity of the concept of equality.

The *evil* of slavery was widely granted, in the South as well as the North; *the political use* of the fact of slavery was premised largely on other than moral concerns. The United States was, in the Supreme Court and presidency, largely dominated by the South from its inception until 1860. There is no understanding of the era apart from this fact. One may well wish that slavery had been the moral issue of that time, but it still remains true that an immoral and political use of this moral issue was made by various northern groups, without respect for the consequences to Negro and white. Lincoln was concerned with the federal union more than with slavery, but many Radical Republicans were more concerned with the creation of a national state over the dead body of the South *and* the federal union. The situation facing the country in the 1850s was thus a difficult one.

Other pressing problems had been side-tracked, and the moral issue of slavery subordinated, in terms of a political conflict.

> In the event of the emancipation of slaves there were, in the simplest possible form of analysis, three possibilities from which to choose for the solution of the race question: (1) a mixed racial society; (2) African colonization; (3) white supremacy based upon segregation in one of three forms. To most people, both north and south, the first was unacceptable. The second was highly acceptable, but proved impracticable. As of the 1850s, except for a very few extremists, the solution narrowed down to a choice of forms of segregation, isolation of free negroes, or slavery. Geographical isolation of free negroes took the form of exclusion of free negroes from free states. Manifestly, that was applicable only to a few states and was especially attractive to new territories, but as a general solution was an absurdity because there was no place within the United States for them to be segregated. Either the negro must be moved or the white people emigrate. Isolation might be achieved by the creation of a bi-racial society, and to a certain extent that was being done, but placed the free negro in a subordinate position. Reduced to this order of reality, the negro remained in slavery as the most effective method of segregation even though probably more than eighty per cent of the white population of the slave states were without slaves and there is reason to believe a large part of them were definitely antislavery as a matter of principle.[12]

Lincoln, in his First Inaugural Address, March 4, 1861, stated that his consistent stand had been non-abolitionist:

[12.] Malin, *The Nebraska Question*, 407f. For interesting sidelights on the antislavery crusade, see J. C. Furnas, *The Road to Harpers Ferry* (New York: Sloane, 1959); and Lawrence Lader, *The Bold Brahmins, New England's War Against Slavery, 1831-1863* (New York: Dutton, 1961).

It is found in nearly all the published speeches of him who now addresses you. I do but quote from one of those speeches when I declare that — I have no purpose, directly or indirectly, to interfere with the institution of slavery in the States where it exists. I believe I have no lawful right to do so, and I have no inclination to do so.

The people had, he held, the *"constitutional* right" of amending their form of government "or the *revolutionary* right to dismember or overthrow it," but apparently not of "civil war."

The South chose to fire. Scott urged adoption of the Anaconda Plan, whereby the South would be forced back into the Union within a year by economic blockade and without bloodshed. The Radical Republicans, however, wanted not simply war, but a prolonged war of attrition and the reduction of the South, followed by its humiliation. Lincoln acceded to these ideas, changing his views toward Reconstruction only towards the end.[13]

On July 17, 1862, "An Act to suppress insurrection, to punish treason and rebellion, to seize and confiscate the property of rebels, and for other purposes" made provision "for the transportation, colonization, and settlement, in some tropical country beyond the limits of the United States, of such persons of the African race, made free by the provisions of this act, as may be willing to emigrate." On September 22, 1862, Lincoln declared that the Colonization effort would be continued and further implemented by legislation. In his second annual message, December 1, 1862, Lincoln asked for money to carry out the already approved colonization of negroes and noted that "some would retain them with us." The matter was a subject of a communication on March 12, 1864, Lincoln sending the Senate a report of funds expended for colonization.[14] Earlier, April 16, 1863, a Haiti colonization plan, signed by Lincoln, was voided because the U.S. Seal was not affixed and Lincoln had subsequent doubts as to aspects of that plan. The Emancipation Proclamation must be set in this context of colonization hopes. However illusory, they were a long-standing consideration and were legally enacted by Congress. The Negro was to be emancipated from slavery, and, many hoped and believed, the United States was to be emancipated of the Negro. As late as March, 1865, a month before his assassination, Lincoln was considering the removal of the entire Negro population from the United States.[15]

Andrew Johnson, in his First Annual Message, December 4, 1865, suggested another approach:

13. See Otto Eisenschiml, *The Hidden Face of the Civil War* (Indianapolis: Bobbs-Merrill, 1961).
14. James D. Richardson, ed., *A Compilation of the Messages and Papers of the Presidents*, vol. VI (Washington D.C., 1904), 96, 136, 167, 200.
15. Nathaniel Weyl, *The Negro in American Civilization* (Washington, D.C.: Public Affairs Press, 1960), 78.

The country is in need of labor, and the freedmen are in need of employment, culture, and protection. While their right of voluntary migration and expatriation is not to be questioned, I would not advise their forced removal and colonization. Let us rather encourage them to honorable and useful industry, where it may be beneficial to themselves and to the country; and, instead of hasty anticipations of the certainty of failure, let there be nothing wanting to the fair trial of the experiment.[16]

Many churchmen and Union generals dedicated themselves to the cause of the freedmen. The Radical Republicans were more concerned, however, with using the Negro as a weapon for bludgeoning the South. Johnson, himself a Southerner, spoke apparently with an eye on both the South and on the interventionist financial powers associated with the Radical Republicans, when he continued:

Now that slavery is at an end, or near its end, the greatness of its evil in the point of view of public economy becomes more and more apparent. Slavery was essentially a monopoly, of labor, and as such locked the States where it prevailed against the incoming of free industry. Where labor was the property of the capitalist, the white man was excluded from employment, or had but the second best chance of finding it; and the foreign emigrant turned away from the region where his condition would be so precarious. With the destruction of the monopoly free labor will hasten from all parts of the civilized world to assist in developing various and immeasurable resources which have hitherto lain dormant. The eight or nine States nearest the Gulf of Mexico have a soil of exuberant fertility, a climate friendly to long life, and can sustain a denser population than is found as yet in any part of our country. And the future influx of population to them will be mainly from the North or from the most cultivated nations in Europe. From the sufferings that have attended them during our late struggle let us look away to the future, which is sure to be laden for them with greater prosperity than has ever before been known. The removal of the monopoly of slave labor is a pledge that those regions will be peopled by a numerous and enterprising population, which will vie with any in the Union in compactness, inventive genius, wealth, and industry.

...Here there is no room for favored classes or monopolies; the principle of our Government is that of equal laws and freedom of industry. Wherever monopoly attains a foothold, it is sure to be a source of danger, discord, and trouble. We shall but fulfill our duties as legislators by according "equal and exact justice to all men," special privileges to none. The Government is subordinate to the people; but, as the agent and representative of the people, it must be held superior to monopolies, which in themselves ought never to be granted, and

[16.] Richardson, 360. This message was "written by the historian George Bancroft," Benjamin P. Thomas and Harold M. Hyman, *Stanton, The Life and Times of Lincoln's Secretary of War* (New York: Alfred A. Knopf, 1962), 464. On Bancroft, see Russel B. Nye, *George Bancroft, Brahmin Rebel* (New York: Alfred A. Knopf, 1945).

which, where they exist, must be subordinate and yield to the Government.[17]

Translated into present-day terminology, this would imply that Johnson did not believe in *either* legal segregation *or* legal integration, being opposed to monopolistic use of law. Likewise, no economic group, corporate business or labor, could expect a legal position based upon favoritism, in that this would constitute monopoly. At the beginning of his administration, in April, 1865, Johnson said, to an Indiana delegation, that, "while I have opposed dissolution and disintegration on the one hand, on the other I am equally opposed to consolidation, or the centralization of power in the hands of a few."[18]

The colonization hope continued with many, and, on June 16, 1866, Johnson supplied, in answer to a Senate resolution "information touching the transactions of the executive branch of the Government respecting the transportation, settlement, and colonization of persons of the African race."[19]

In his veto message of February 19, 1866, Johnson spoke sharply concerning the raids on the treasury in the name of suffering Negroes. He denied that the Constitution gave any ground for such legislation for any or all classes and races.

> A system for the support of indigent persons in the United States was never contemplated by the authors of the Constitution; nor can any good reason be advanced why, as a permanent establishment, it should be founded for one class or color of our people more than another. Pending the war many refugees and freedmen received support from the Government, but it was never intended that they should thenceforth be fed, clothed, educated, and sheltered by the United States. The idea on which the slaves were assisted to freedom was that on becoming free they would be a self-sustaining population. Any legislation that shall imply that they are not expected to attain a self-sustaining condition must have a tendency injurious alike to their character and their prospects....The appropriations asked by the Freedmen's Bureau as now established, for the year 1866, amount to $11,745,000. It may be safely estimated that the cost to be incurred under the pending bill will require double that amount—more than the entire sum expended in any one year under the Administration of the second Adams.[20]

On March 27, 1866, Johnson expressed to the Senate in a Veto Message his strong dissent in relation to an act making federal citizens of all Negroes

---

[17.] Richardson, 361f.

[18.] Frank Moore, ed., *Speeches of Andrew Johnson, President of the United States* (Boston: Little, Brown, 1866), 484.

[19.] Richardson, 390.

[20.] *Ibid.*, 401.

(and also Pacific States Chinese) against all normal requirements of citizenship.

> Four million of them have just emerged from slavery into freedom. Can it be reasonably supposed that they possess the requisite qualifications to entitle them to all the privileges and immunities of citizens of the United States? Have the people of the several States expressed such a conviction?...The bill in effect proposes a discrimination against large numbers of intelligent, worthy, and patriotic foreigners, and in favor of the negro, to whom, after long years of bondage, the avenues of freedom and intelligence have just now been suddenly opened. He must of necessity, from his previous unfortunate condition of servitude, be less informed as to the nature and character of our institutions than he who, coming from abroad, has, to some extent at least, familiarized himself with the principles of a Government to which he voluntarily intrusts "life, liberty, and the pursuit of happiness."[21]

The rights of the States to determine citizenship were being invaded, Johnson held. "Laws of discrimination" with respect to real estate, suits, contracts, and marriage were the general rule; some of these were probably unconstitutional, but their remedy was not further unconstitutional action. "The legislation thus proposed invades the judicial power of the States."[22] Johnson recognized that the congressional concern was not the Negro but the destruction of the South as a *means* to the erection of a *national statist order*.

> It is another step, or rather stride, toward centralization and the concentration of all legislative power in the National Government. The tendency of the bill must be to resuscitate the spirit of rebellion and to arrest the progress of those influences which are most closely drawing around the States the bonds of union and peace. [23]

The same point was again made in a Veto Message of January 5, 1867, with reference to "An act to regulate the elective franchise in the District of Columbia." To grant suffrage to people unprepared to exercise it could only lead to one quite obvious end: "Controlled through fraud and usurpation by the designing, anarchy and despotism must inevitably follow."[24]

---

[21] *Ibid.*, 406.

[22] *Ibid.*, 409.

[23] *Ibid.*, 413.

[24] *Ibid.*, 478. Note Gideon Welles' comment on the race riots of July 30, 1866, in New Orleans: "Stanton read telegrams in Cabinet from General Sheridan concerning New Orleans disturbances. Stanton manifested marked sympathy with the rioters, and the President and others observed it. There is little doubt that the New Orleans riots had their origin with the Radical Members of Congress in Washington. It [is part of a deliberate conspiracy and] was to be the commencement of a series of bloody affrays through the States lately in rebellion." Howard K. Beale, ed., *Diary of Gideon Welles*, vol. II (New York: Norton, 1960), 569. Material in brackets was Welles' own addition.

In his Third Annual Message, December 3, 1867, Johnson, a dedicated constitutionalist, posed the question clearly and simply. "The Union and the Constitution are inseparable....To me the process of restoration seems perfectly plain and simple. It consists merely in a faithful application of the Constitution and laws."[25] The Constitution provided the best guarantees for all concerned. What was proposed and in process of institution was unconstitutional and racist, calling for the vengeful domination of Southern whites by blacks.

> It is manifestly and avowedly the object of these laws to confer upon negroes the privilege of voting and to disfranchise such a number of white citizens as will give the former a clear majority at all elections in the Southern States. This, to the minds of some persons, is so important that a violation of the Constitution is justified as a means of bringing it about. The morality is always false which excuses a wrong because it proposes to accomplish a desirable end. We are not permitted to do evil that good may come. But in this case the end itself is evil, as well as the means. The subjugation of the States to negro domination would be worse than the military despotism under which they are now suffering. It was believed beforehand that the people would endure any amount of military oppression for any length of time rather than degrade themselves by subjection to the negro race. Therefore they have been left without a choice. Negro suffrage was established by act of Congress, and the military officers were commanded to superintend the process of clothing the negro race with the political privileges torn from white men.
>
> The blacks in the South are entitled to be well and humanely governed, and to have the protection of just laws for all their rights of person and property. If it were practicable at this time to give them a Government exclusively their own, under which they might manage their own affairs in their own way, it would become a grave question whether we ought to do so, or whether common humanity would not require us to save them from themselves. But under the circumstances this is only a speculative point. It is not proposed merely that they shall govern themselves, but that they shall rule the white race, make and administer State laws, elect Presidents and members of Congress, and shape to a greater or lesser extent the future destiny of the whole country. Would such a trust and power be safe in such hands?[26]
>
> But if anything can be proved by known facts, if all reasoning upon evidence *is* not abandoned, it must be acknowledged that in the progress of nations negroes have shown less capacity for government than any other race of people. No independent government of any form has ever been successful in their hands. On the contrary, wherever they have been left to their own devices they have shown a constant tendency to relapse into barbarism. In the Southern States,

---

25. Richardson, 559.
26. *Ibid.*, 564.

however, Congress has undertaken to confer upon them the privilege of the ballot.[27]

What was proposed, Johnson declared, was the creation of "such a tyranny as this continent has never yet witnessed." It was a design to "Africanize the half of our country" and by military force maintain the racial supremacy of the Negro at a cost capable of reducing "the nation to a condition of bankruptcy." Together with this program was the degradation of money, in that paper money had been made legal tender. The result was that bad money was driving out good money and was, in the process, robbing the laboring classes. Paper money was the legalized destruction of the working man and of virtue to the profit "of the few."[28] Powerful financial interests, to whom the U. S. Government was only a tool for the robbing of the people, were in control, and Johnson was an obstruction.

The background to this movement was a complex one. The American Democracy Party, which, after Jackson's day, was the party of compromise, became, with the Republican triumph, the party hostile to all compromise and thereby pushed for war, standing now, however, not on principle but on the vested interests of a slaveholding aristocracy. Johnson's attempt to compromise tensions and restore constitutional principles thus clashed with both Southern intransigence and Northern, Radical Republican hostility to all compromise. The Radical Republicans opposed any restoration of the South to its proper status in the Union since such a move would make the Republicans a minority party. Thus, the North fought to preserve the Union and to keep the South from leaving it, but, having won, refused to permit the South to be in it except in the form of puppet governments. More than the Civil War intervened between the first half of the century and Johnson. Darwin's concept of evolution was responsible for a great revolution of thought. The conservative merchants, farmers, bankers, planters, and others who predominated until 1860 were supplanted by a new breed, no longer "adherents of old-fashioned Christianity" but social Darwinists. The old order was overthrown by "a great domestic tragedy that synchronized chronologically with an intellectual revolution overseas."[29] Andrew Carnegie expressed the receptiveness of this new order to Darwin in his *Autobiography*, describing his reading of Darwin and Spencer: "I remember that light came as in a flood and all was clear. Not only had I got rid of theology and the supernatural, but I had found the truth of evolution. 'All is well since all

---

27. *Ibid.*, 565.
28. *Ibid.*, 566f., 571-574. For an able evaluation of Johnson, see Lloyd Paul Stryker, *Andrew Johnson, A Study in Courage* (New York: Macmillan, 1929).
29. Charles McArthur Destler, "Entrepreneurial Leadership Among the 'Robber Barons', A Trial Balance," in Sidney Fine and Gerald S. Brown, *The American Past*, vol. II (New York: Macmillan, 1961), 43.

grows better' became my motto, my true source of comfort."[30] Morality was now not a matter of personal relationship to and growth in Christ, but of biological process, inevitable and hence not personal. Carnegie, coming from a background of French revolutionary thought and Chartism, now found his bent scientifically "confirmed." Other "capitalists" of this new order followed in the same pattern of thought; morality ceased to be a matter of character: since all is well, or legitimate, because of necessary and biological growth, then limitations on man are obsolete.

The South was accordingly plundered by American and foreign financial and industrial interests, with the help of puppet governments and many Southern financial and industrial groups. The Union League organized Negroes into secret societies to further its domination and exploitation of the South, and savagely fought Johnson in Washington. What was championed in the name of capitalism and Radical Republicanism was actually interventionism and socialism, class socialism, the class favored being the financial interests. The New York Union League Club could boast, in 1887 (Chauncey M. Depew then being its president), that "To the Union League Club was largely due the impelling force which carried through the Reconstruction Acts, and put into the Constitution of the United States in permanent and enduring form the results won upon our battlefields." It could confidently, and with reason, assert, in discussing "Its Future," that "There is no State or National Convention of the Republican Party which dares put before the country nominees who would receive its disapprobation, because that would be the damnation of the ticket."[31] In the selection of McKinley at a later date, the Chicago Union League Club and its member, Charles Gates Dawes, took primary credit.[32]

Prior to the Civil War, although a radical ferment was apparent in the 1840s, the character of American life was not collectivistic or individualistic. It was Christian, familistic, and personal; a sense of community, personal and familistic, generally prevailed. Evolutionary thought emphasized impersonal process, and the cities, previously

---

[30.] Edward C. Kirkland, "Introduction," in Andrew Carnegie, *The Gospel of Wealth, and Other Timely Essays* (Cambridge: Harvard University Press, 1962), xi. Carnegie opposed the hereditary transmission of wealth but favored its use "during the life-time of its possessors" for the benefit of all in charitable and educational activities, so that "the wealth of the few will become in the best sense the property of the many, because administered for the common good"; A. Carnegie, "The Heredity Transmissions of Property," *The Century Magazine*, 87, no. 3 (January, 1914),441-443. Darwinism was the economic law; charity aimed at re-fitting the weak.

[31.] See F. N. Thorpe, ed., *The History of North America*, vol. XVI, Peter Joseph Hamilton, *The Reconstruction Period* (Philadelphia: Barrie, 1905), 405-430. See also Claude G. Bowers, *The Tragic Era* (Boston: Houghton Mifflin, 1962). See especially E. Merton Coulter, *The South During Reconstruction, 1865-1877* (Baton Rouge: Louisiana State University Press, 1947)

[32.] Bruce Grant, *Fight for a City, The Story of the Union League Club of Chicago and its Times, 1880-1955* (Chicago: Rand McNally, 1955), 152ff.

governed by a Christian concept of government and community, now became sanctuaries of impersonalism. Truly rational man meant impersonal and rootless man,[33] and the cities, even after the development of roadways and ease of transportation made them economically less advantageous to industry than decentralized industrial development, continued to grow because they met a psychological need. The flight from personalism and responsibility, from roots and from history, meant a flight to the city. Corporate and statist impersonalism and collectivism grew simultaneously with "rugged individualism," an anarchistic and impersonal individualism which moved in contempt of personal, moral, and Christian considerations. The so-called "66 capitalists" were often socialistic in terms of their presuppositions, government manipulators, who believed in the principle of class legislation and state controls towards that end. Their point of difference with Marxism was in part a question of power: which class would control the state? Aspects of such government manipulation existed prior to the Civil War, especially as a result of the constitutional provision for a federal postal service. This ostensibly innocent provision led to extensive subsidies to railroad and steamship corporations and created a new and powerful class whose wealth rested on government subsidies, manipulations, and even outright fraudulent practices, as the Covode investigation indicated. The results were disastrous for both the character of federal government and that of American life. It is not surprising that Savage has termed this period following the Civil War the "Second American Revolution," and "a revolution in which most of the rebels were numbered among the Yankees."[34] To maintain this Revolution, it was necessary to prevent the restoration of civil rights to the South, and also to eliminate Johnson. Johnson's resistance was a major aspect of the history of constitutionalism. Southerners were of little help to Johnson, in that, then and later, they were ready to use all the practices of "carpetbag" government for their own benefit, including the toleration of Negro suffrage if it remained subject to their control. Johnson's position was thus a difficult one.

In a Veto Message on "An act to admit the State of Arkansas to representation in Congress," June 20, 1868, Johnson called attention to Article 8, Section 5, of that act, requiring that "all persons, before registering or voting," take an oath which contained the following clause:

[33.] See R. J. Rushdoony, *The Messianic Character of American Education* (Nutley, N.J.: Craig Press, 1963).

[34.] Savage, 140. James C. Malin says that "a unitary national revolution was in the making," *On the Nature of History, Essays about History and Dissidence* (Ann Arbor, Mich.: J. W. Edwards, 1954), 203. For Henry Adams' discussion of the powers of corporate bodies in this situation, see H. Adams, "The New York Gold Conspiracy," in his *The Great Secession Winter of 1860-61 and Other Essays*, edited by George Hochfield (New York: Sagamore Press, 1958), 157-189.

That I accept the civil and political equality of all men, and agree not to attempt to deprive any person or persons, on account of race, color, or previous condition, of any political or civil right, privilege, or immunity enjoyed by any other class of men.

Johnson called attention to the fact that this clause was inserted in the face of the known fact "that a very large portion of the electors" did not believe in it. "Is it intended that a denial of representation should follow?" Was it not likely that such measures would only lay the groundwork for future trouble?[35]

In his Fourth Annual Message, December 9, 1868, Johnson returned to the monetary problem.[36] The answer to Johnson's conscientious and able constitutionalism was, on a specious charge with reference to Stanton, an impeachment attempt. His resolute struggle to deal with issues constitutionally has gone largely unappreciated. Even conservatives like Garrett have dismissed him as "a man who had the common misfortune to be born without wisdom."[37] Despite many defeats, Johnson did hinder at points and prevent at others a flagrant statist reordering of the United States. The damage done, however, was real. And, in the South, whereas the Negro had nominal assistance from the Freedmen's Bureau, the non-slaveholding white yeomanry emerged from this era extensively impoverished and embittered. And this meant the impoverishment of most of the South, for only one of every sixteen Southerners had owned even a single slave.[38]

In all this, genuine concern for the Negro had been very slight. A Negro editor in Charleston, Richard Harvey Cain, in 1871 observed, "When the smoke and fighting is over, the negroes have gained nothing and the whites have nothing left, while the jackals have all the booty."[39] Abolitionist leaders showed more hate than love on the whole. It was not surprising then that, after the use of the Negro as a political bludgeon against the Southern white, there was a readiness to allow the Southerner a free hand *on the condition* of political concessions, so that the South became a political ally of Republican forces ready to concede its freedom in this respect. At first, the Negro received better treatment in the South than in the North.[40]Southern Populism began by resolving to "wipe out the color line, and put every man on his citizenship irrespective of color," to cite Tom Watson's words, and only gradually turned to racism.[41] The Southern

35. Richardson, 650.
36. *Ibid.*, 672-682.
37. Garet Garrett, *The American Story* (Chicago: Regnery, 1955), 115.
38. Savage, 86. On the Freedmen's Bureau's work, see Hamilton, *The Reconstruction Period*, 429f.
39. E. Merton Coulter, *The South During Reconstruction*, 159.
40. Weyl, *The Negro in American Civilization*, 108.

Negro was now the object of prejudicial legislation, while all Southerners suffered through discriminatory railroad rates, allegedly imposed by the financial interests controlling the railroads.[42] When the Negro became a better potential tool than the Southern white, and his northern migrations made him a political factor, he was again made the object of political use in the 1930s and thereafter. Thus, in a century's time, the Negro exchanged slavery to an individual for slavery to the State. In both conditions, there are advantages, but both constitute slavery.

Whatever the political or legal picture has been, the honest fact is that, for the most part, the white American has *not* felt much sense of unity or equality with the Negro. Compassion, charity, kindliness, friendliness, bitterness, resentment, hatred, and exploitation, these things have all existed, but the sense of unity or equality has been virtually absent. Neither Jefferson nor Lincoln can be cited as champions of anything resembling unity or equality. Cooper denied the validity of the concept of equality.[43] The existence of *government* and *property* alike militated against equality, in that both instituted differences among men. Moreover,

> Equality is no where laid down as a governing principle of the institutions of the United States, neither the word, nor any inference that can be fairly deduced from its meaning, occurring in the constitution....

> Desirable in practice, it can hardly be, since the result would be to force all down to the level of the lowest....All that a good government aims at, therefore, is to add no unnecessary and artificial aid to the force of its own unavoidable consequences, and to abstain from fortifying and accumulating social inequality as a means of increasing political inequalities.[44]

For Cooper, the American federal system was a better guarantee of man's liberty than the general professions of other countries. He felt that the majoritarian principles of France made it basically hostile to liberty, and that "the government of Great Britain, which, though freer in practice than that of France, is not based on a really free system."[45]

A concerted effort has been made in recent years to introduce equality into the United States as a political goal. The Boas school of anthropology has sought to give it a scientific foundation, a position which has gained

---

[41.] C. Vann Woodward, *Tom Watson, Agrarian Rebel* (New York: Macmillan, 1938), 231.
[42.] See, for this continuing pattern, John G. Shott, *The Railroad Monopoly, An Instrument of Banker Control of the American Economy* (Washington, D.C.: Public Affairs Institute, 1950).
[43.] Cooper, *The American Democrat*, 43ff.
[44.] *Ibid.*, 47.
[45.] *Ibid.*, 54.

widespread support, although with some dissent arising in recent years.[46]The South, however, has sought legally to perpetuate segregation. The basic issue is too seldom raised: are not both legalized integration and segregation interferences with freedom of association?

In terms of the reality of the Negro's presence in America, and his growing participation in American hopes, two solutions, in the main, are possible. The first is the statist answer. *The sense of corporateness* is sought on the "national" level (or, with some, on an international level). Persons and groups will not be allowed any divisive practices or racial freedom of choice, all of which will be, or are in process of being, banned by law. Creedal or religious differences are likewise being proscribed. There must be a total unity in terms of the state, and hence internal differences must be suppressed.

Corporateness on the state level will, however, destroy all corporateness on the personal, institutional, and group levels, so that no solution to the personal fact will ensue. Enforced uniformity, it is assumed, will in time produce unity, but the price of that unity will be the suppression of liberty and individuality. In addition, the statist sense of corporateness requires the destruction of federalism and constitutionalism, and thus this same sense of corporateness is denied to the federal union, and, to a lesser extent, to state and country.

The second answer is thus indicated. The sense of corporateness was denied by the Constitution and the federal structure to the political bodies and made *personal and societal*. The establishment of any church by Congress was forbidden as one aspect of this reservation of the right of association and of corporateness. The noncorporate nature of the federal union ensured a free society; the corporateness of the local units and groups made possible *closed groups* in terms of particular faiths, races, and classes. This is an *inevitable choice: if the corporateness of the state is demanded, individual corporateness and freedom are destroyed.* Deny the corporateness

---

[46.] See Roger J. Williams, *Free and Unequal, the Biological Basis of Individual Liberty* (Austin: University of Texas Press, 1953); see also Carleton Putnam, *Race and Reason, A Yankee View* (Washington, D.C.: Public Affairs Press, 1961); Weyl's study, *The Negro in American Civilization,* is the most comprehensive. The Christian case against racism, by a Southern negro, is ably presented, despite a tendency to rely on statist measures, by C. Herbert Oliver, *No Flesh Shall Glory* (Philadelphia: Presbyterian and Reformed, 1959). For an important Southern statement, see William D. Workman Jr., *The Case for the South* (New York: Devin-Adair, 1960). See also J. C. Furnas' valuable analysis, *Goodbye to Uncle Tom* (New York: Sloane, 1956). For the current attempt to give a legal answer to the problem, see Davis McEntire, *Residence and Race, Final and Comprehensive Report to the Commission on Race and Housing* (Berkeley: University of California Press, 1960). For conflicting scientific perspectives, see Carleton S. Coon, *The Origin of Races* (New York: Knopf, 1963); M. F. Ashley Montagu, *Man's Most Dangerous Myth: The Fallacy of Race* (New York: Columbia University Press, 1942); "'Scientific' Racism Again?," *Current Anthropology* (October, 1961), 303-340. See for a further aspect, John Caravan, "Freedom of Association," *Man and the State,* 1, no. 3 (29 March 1963), 2.

of the state, and, on the local level, the reality of prejudices and divisions must be faced, and they can militate against Negro, Protestant, Roman Catholic, Jew, college graduate, alien, or anyone else. The free development of local corporateness is, moreover, the very necessary agency of its growth and of incorporation. It will also create a demand for the responsible development of groups or persons seeking status within society. Thus pride, responsible achievement, and self-respect, function rather than legal encroachment, as means to advancement. Legalism is a Procrustean bed, and is not only in violation of but also destructive to natural growth. Hints of the possibility of such a free development have been forthcoming of late from the South.[47]

The American position had its origins in English Separatism, which early denied the validity in principle of the legalistic approach to religion. Henry Barrow, Separatist and martyr (1550?-1593), shepherd and theologian to the Pilgrim Fathers, was accused on examination of two particular things. First, he was charged with rebellion against authority. He resented this charge, and any allegation of Anabaptism. "There is not a sentence in our writings," he declared, which hints at absolute independence of "the Superior Powers that God hath set over us." Rather, they sought for the establishment of true authority in terms of God's word. Second, he was charged with seeking to level or equalize. Barrow denied this strongly. The church is indeed a brotherhood, a communion of saints, but "though there be communion in the Church yet there is no equality."[48] *Communion, not equality,* was the original and Christian concept of society in America, and the effects of this concept have long lingered. They underlie and require a federal and constitutional structure. Communion is a religious concept. Equality as it is often championed today is a rationalistic and scientific abstraction, a concept best promulgated in French revolutionary thought. Basic to this concept of equality is a utopianism, a *desire to end history* and an intolerance for the very human fact of problems and tensions. The religious concept of communion describes history as both conflict and development, and sees as necessary the *integrity* of communion and its growth in terms of a supernatural calling and law. The focal point of true unity cannot be racial but must be Jesus Christ. And the community of Christ cannot be used as a weapon of social change, but is rather a place of Christian growth: "Let every man abide in the same calling wherein he was called" (1 Cor. 7:20). Man's hope is not primarily in civil law and social change but in Christ, not to be realized in dead "works" but through a

---

47. See Leon Dure, "The New Southern Response: Anatomy of Two New Free-doms," *The Georgia Review*, 15, no. 4 (Winter, 1961), 401-416.
48. F. J. Powicke, *Henry Barrow, Separatist and the Exiled Church of Amsterdam, 1593-1622* (London: Clark, 1900), 94, 128.

living and working faith, itself of grace, in Jesus Christ the Lord. As Malin has observed:

> Whatever effect the revolutionary philosophers of the late eighteenth century may have had in modification of religion in the United States, the core of the Christian plan of Salvation survived, regardless of denomination—men could not save themselves; they could find Salvation only through Divine intervention—the Blood Sacrifice. Christianity and the generalized Idea of Progress were irreconcilable.[49]

In this Christian pattern, the integrity of differences was recognized. In the New Testament, there is neither segregation nor integration. Jewish converts organized Jewish churches, and Gentiles their own congregations, without barring one another. Each was to develop in terms of his history and tradition within the framework of Christ's body. Community, not uniformity, was the emphasis. "To prevent the Jew from remaining a Jew, would be to abolish freedom and to reintroduce a law into the Church. That is why Paul always opposed uniformity in the Church."[50] The modern, anti-Biblical answer is environmentalistic: change man's conditions, and his character will be changed. As Harry Golden has stated it, with reference to the Negro, "The first thing is freedom; responsibility follows."[51]

The early American solution to problems was neither collectivism nor individualism but rather Christianity. The sense of community was thus basic. This made for a slower solution to problems, but a more basic one. As problems arose, men voluntarily associated themselves in missionary, educational, charitable, and other associations in order to deal with the situation. One of the results of such activity was the major missionary movement of all church history, another the greatest educational advance into higher education up to 1900. These were not statist movements; they were the outcome of voluntary associations.

Tocqueville noted that the Americans, having a Constitution which was anti-statist, sought to combat the other tendency, *individualism,* by means of *associations.* Associations forestalled statist action and prevented the atomism of individualism. "Wherever, at the head of some new undertaking, you see the government in France, or a man of rank in England, in the United States you will be sure to find an association."[52]

---

49. Malin, *The Contriving Brain and the Skillful Hand,* 16.

50. Adolph Schlatter, *The Church in the New Testament Period* (London: SPCK, 1961), 207. See also Jean Danielou, S.J., *The Lord of History, Reflections on the Inner Meaning of History* (Chicago: Regnery, 1958), 58.

51. Harry Golden, "Only in America: 'The Negro Revolt,'" *New York Post,* 15 October 1962, 29.

52. Alexis de Tocqueville, *Democracy in America,* vol. II (New York: Langley, 1841), 114.

Tocqueville, in commenting on the tendency of democracy to concentrate political power, added, in a footnote:

> Men connect the greatness of their idea of unity with means, God with ends; hence this idea of greatness, as men conceive it, leads us into infinite littleness. To compel all men to follow the same course toward the same object is a human notion;—to introduce infinite variety of action, but so combined that all these acts lead by a multitude of different courses to the accomplishment of one great design, is a conception of the Deity.
>
> The human idea of unity is almost always barren; the divine idea pregnant with abundant results. Men think they manifest their greatness by simplifying the means they use; but it is the purpose of God which is simple—his means are infinitely varied.[53]

The "democratic" sentiment some scholars see in the American Revolution was generally a religious product, a sense of communion and community. Thus, Miller has called attention to "New England levelism" and the "democratic" attitudes of the Scotch-Irish farmers and immigrants of that era.[54] In the New England regiments, "a large part of the officers were farmers and the sons of farmers, who hardly pretended to gentility."[55] There was a conflict between these officers and those representing a Church of England background. Even Washington at this point felt required to check "the officers of the New Jersey line for mingling up their grievances with those of the men. Common soldiers, he thought, could not reasonably expect anything more than food and clothing. That was all they received in other armies; their pay, by reason of the numerous deductions to which it was subject, being little more than nominal. Washington regarded as an expensive anomaly the plan adopted in New England and some other states, of providing for the families of soldiers."[56]

The democratic sentiment that captured Pennsylvania from 1776 to 1784, was according to Miller, not so much democratic as religious, Calvinistic, Presbyterian, a belief in communion, the levelling of men before God by faith, and not in terms of the modern concept of equality. This same Christian temper permeated New England, as well as other areas.

Democratic ideas did enter in much later, but even then, much of what is called the progress of democracy was actually the extension of evangelical and Arminian Christianity in nineteenth century America.

The country was, as Cooper saw, very highly undemocratic, but revivalism extended a catholic faith throughout the country and opened up

---

[53.] *Ibid.*, 312.
[54.] John C. Miller, *Origins of the American Revolution*, rev. ed. (Stanford, Calif.: Stanford University Press, 1959), 503f.
[55.] Hildreth, *The History of the United States*, vol. III, 147.
[56.] *Ibid.*, 339.

strong lines of communication and a new variety of the Christian sense of community. This sense of community was often narrow and hostile to outsiders, but also often generous and hospitable. Its virtues were great, and its defects very real. But there can be no strong sense of community without a sense also of the sanctity and integrity of the community. (In the South today, both Negroes and whites have a stronger sense of community than do Negroes and whites in most areas of the United States.) The tremendous possibilities inherent in the development of true community require a readiness to accept the limitations of historical process and maturation. To destroy the sense of community is not only to destroy liberty, but also the Christian church. As Tocqueville noted, statism seeks not only to keep men in a state of "perpetual childhood," but also to use the church, if not to destroy it.[57]

The question then is this: will corporateness be statist, or will it be free and Christian? Will it be an aspect of community life, or will it be a doctrine of State?[58] The pattern of state enforced segregation is clearly statist and a denial of free association, but the demand for coercive integration is no less statist and a denial of the true sources of community.[59]

In 1875, the Rev. Edward Cleveland expressed his faith in progress through freedom "in the field of strife":

> But still, while man in freedom makes his way,
> Some good develops oft from day to day;
> Secures advancement in the field of strife
> While dipping oars upon the stream of life.
> While under ban we only see the dwarf,
> As men seem pigmies on the distant wharf.
> But give full scope to man's unshackled soul,
> To think and speak and judge without control;
> And great development of mind will rise,
> And great achievements will the world surprise.
> Then will the mind throughout creation soar,
> And wonders of the universe explore;
> Inventions make, to aid the human race
> In things substantial and aesthetic grace.
> Religion gains its utmost purity,
> When its development is wholly free.[60]

[57.] Tocqueville, 325, 339.

[58.] For modern developments of the emphasis on local community life, see Arthur E. Morgan, *The Community of the Future and the Future of Community* (Yellow Springs, Ohio: Community Services, Inc., 1957), and his other works. Morgan's work is important although defective theologically. For a study of regionalism in American life, see Donald Davidson, *The Attack on Leviathan, Regionalism and Nationalism in the United States* (Gloucester, Mass.: Peter Smith, 1962).

[59.] See Leon Dure, "Freedom of Association: Laying the Foundation for Racial Peace," *The Roanoke* (Virginia) *Times*, 23 September 1962, A6. A stimulating study is Robert E. Nisbet's *The Quest for Community* (New York: Oxford University Press, 1953).

[60.] Rev. Edward Cleveland, *Bible Sketches, or The Stream of Time* (Boston: Mudge, 1875), 280f.

8

The Holy Commonwealth

When Tocqueville's *Democracy in America* was published in the United States, the English translator added a note to the chapter, "Of Individualism in Democratic Countries," to explain the word "individualism":

> I adopt the expression of the original, however strange it may seem to the English ear, partly because it illustrates the remark on the introduction of general terms into democratic language which was made in a preceding chapter, and partly because I know of no English word exactly equivalent to the expression. The chapter itself defines the meaning attached to it by the author.[1]

The word, from the French *individualisme*, was, as Tocqueville recognized, alien to the United States, and the principle involved in the word an object of hostility. In a subsequent chapter, he described how "The Americans Combat Individualism by the Principle of Interest Rightly Understood":

> The Americans, on the contrary, are fond of explaining almost all the actions of their lives by the principle of interest rightly understood; they show with complacency how an enlightened regard for themselves constantly prompts them to assist each other, and inclines them willingly to sacrifice a portion of their time and property to the welfare of the state.[2]

[1.] Alexis de Tocqueville, *Democracy in America*, vol. II (New York: Langley, 1841), 104.
[2.] *Ibid.*, 130.

As Tocqueville saw it, individualism is brought into being in part and caused to flourish by democracy, with its levelling influence, which then destroys individualism:

> Thus not only does democracy make every man forget his ancestors, but it hides his descendants, and separates his contemporaries, from him; it throws him back for ever upon himself alone, and threatens in the end to confine him entirely within the solitude of his own heart.[3]

Non-Christian individualism and democracy erode societal forms, ties, and institutions, and finally leave only the lonely and atomistic individual before the power of the democratic state, which then destroys that individual.

What is the meaning of individualism? It is, first of all, that doctrine or practice which holds that the chief end of society is the promotion of individual welfare, and that this constitutes also the end and purpose of moral law, in other words, that society exists for the sake of its individual members. Second, it is theory or policy having primary and essential regard for individual rights, asserting that the political and economic independence of individual initiative, action, and interest overrules all other concerns, that, politically, the state exits for the individual, and, economically, *laissez faire* must prevail.[4] Individualism is thus in sharp opposition and contrast to the Reformation belief in the priesthood of all believers, which is a covenantal doctrine. Priesthood holds to the centrality of the sovereignty of God. Man is called to serve this sovereign in the Kingdom of God in terms of a threefold office, as priest, prophet, and king under God. As king, he is to exercise dominion in the name of God over all creation; as prophet, he is to interpret all things in terms of the sovereign word of God; as priest, he is to dedicate all things to his sovereign, God. The sovereignty of man in individualism is denied by faith in the sovereignty of God. The secular doctrine of *laissez faire* is a compromise version of the Reformed doctrine of sphere law and of the Enlightenment concept of preestablished harmony, a tenet closely linked to later philosophical anarchism. When Tocqueville wrote, the United States was as yet alien to individualism, although its seeds were present here and there, and fostered earlier by Jacobins. Its limited but noisy presence was stridently asserted in the Chardon Street Convention of the Friends of Universal Reform in 1840. It became an increasingly vocal aspect of

---

[3.] *Ibid.*, 106.

[4.] See Dagobert D. Runes, ed., *Dictionary of Philosophy*, fifteenth ed., revised (New York: Philosophical Library, 1960), 145. A third meaning of individualism is now developing, individualism as an antonym to collectivism. In this context, it is becoming a conservative and Christian affirmation. It is herein discussed in its historic sense. It should be noted that Puritanism, while not holding to the philosophy of individualism, developed strong individuals and "demanded more of the individual than it did of the church," Edmund S. Morgan, *The Puritan Dilemma, The Story of John Winthrop* (Boston: Little, Brown, 1958), 7.

American life and sought to read the history of the republic in terms of *rugged individualism.* The expression as well as the philosophy of rugged individualism derived, first, from English and continental Enlightenment thinkers and French revolutionary sources, and, second, from Darwinianism, the application of these earlier ideas to science and through science back again to philosophy, history, economics, political science, education, and religion. What had characterized Americans previously, and continued to govern many, was not individualism, but a sense of destiny as God's *chosen people,* with faith in their calling, not only in terms of the personal covenant of grace, and as a church covenant and the development of the Reformation, but also as a *civil* covenant, a called people of God as a civil order, surrounded by the notable and marvellous tokens of His providence. Timothy Dwight's *Conquest of Canaan* (1785) is eloquent evidence of this faith. *The Federalist* also assumed the same role of Providence, as witness Jay in no. 2. Hamilton saw God's hand in the federal convention and in the Revolution: "It is impossible for the man of pious reflection not to perceive in it a finger of that Almighty hand which has so frequently and signally extended to our relief in the critical stages of the revolution."[5] In his First Inaugural Address, April 30, 1789, Washington stated that it would be "improper" to neglect God or "fervent supplications" to Him. "No people can be bound to acknowledge and adore the Invisible Hand which conducts the affairs of men more than those of the United States. Every step by which they have advanced to the character of an independent nation seems to have been distinguished by some token of providential agency."[6] Timothy Dwight, in "Good Advice in Bad Verse" (1787), saw the restoration of Eden as part of America's destiny and summoned America to "perfect her federal system...for this stupendous realm, this chosen race."[7] A faith in America's providential care and destiny was widely asserted. It is a faith in strong evidence asserted today, as witness the work of a distinguished attorney, T. J. Campbell, *Central Themes of American Life* (1959). The fact that scholars have chosen to ignore it has not made this faith any less a factor.

The sense of holy destiny was early present, and even Englishmen who were temporary residents caught it. Thus, George Berkeley (1685-1753), in his poem "On the Prospect of Planting Arts and Learning in America," declared in conclusion:

---

[5]. *Federalist*, no. 37. For the Puritan roots of Manifest Destiny, note Louis B. Wright, *Culture on the Moving Frontier* (Bloomington: Indiana University Press, 1955), 32.

[6]. James D. Richardson, ed., *A Compilation of the Messages and Papers of the Presidents*, vol. I (Washington D.C.: 1904), 52.

[7]. Albert Bushnell Hart, *American History Told by Contemporaries*, vol. I (New York: MacMillan, 1897), 200-203.

Not such as Europe breeds in her decay:
    Such as she bred when fresh and young,
When heavenly flame did animate her clay,
    By future poets shall be sung.
Westward the course of empire takes its way;
    The first four acts already past,
A fifth shall close the drama with the day;
    Time's noblest offspring is the last.

A former royal governor, Pownall, writing from London, could echo this faith in words informed by Biblical prophecies:

> Being thus planted in a New System in a New World...if they take up this character and hold out its operation and effect to the Old World, they will become a nation *to whom all nations will come,* the oppressed and injured of every nation will seek for refuge. The riches of the sea will pour in upon them; the wealth of nations must flow in upon them.... [8]

In an election sermon of 1783, President Ezra Stiles (1725-1795) of Yale emphasized the Christian destiny of America in terms of Biblical prophecy:

> Heaven has provided this country, not indeed derelict, but only partially settled, and consequently open for the reception of a new enlargement of Japheth. Europe was settled by Japheth; America *is* settling from Europe: and perhaps this second enlargement bids fair to surpass the first.... In two or three hundred years this second enlargement may cover America with (a population of three hundred million).... The United States may be two hundred million souls, whites.... Can we contemplate their present, and anticipate their future increase, and not be struck with astonishment to find ourselves in the midst of the fulfillment of the prophecy of Noah? May we not see that we are the object which the Holy Ghost had in view four thousand years ago, when he inspired the venerable patriarch with the visions respecting his posterity? [9]

The summons to colonize New England had been a religious call in terms of this faith. While it was "more especially" New England, it included "the Westerne World," i.e., of English settlement. Thus, in 1654, Captain Edward Johnson, in *A History of New England, or Wonder-Working Providence of Sion's Saviour,* published in London, declared:

> Christ Jesus intending to manifest his Kingly Office toward his Churches more fully than ever yet the Sons of men saw....stirres up his servants as the Heralds of a King to make this Proclamation for Voluntiers as followeth.

---

8. Thomas Pownall, *A Memorial Addressed to the Sovereigns of Europe on the Present State of Affairs between the Old and New World* (London, 1783), 4.
9. John Wingall Thornton, *The Pulpit of the American Revolution* (Boston: Lothrop, 1876), 405f.

Oh yes! oh yes! All you the people of Christ that are here Oppressed, Imprisoned and scurrilously derided, gather yourselves together, your wifes and little ones, and answer to your several Names as you shall be shipped for his service, in the Westerne World, and more especially for planting the united Collonies of new England; Where you are to attend the service of the King of Kings, upon the divulging of this Proclamation by his Herralds at Armes....

Could Casar so suddenly fetch over fresh forces from Europe to Asia, Pumpy to foyle? How much more shall Christ who createth all power, call over this 900 league Ocean at his pleasure, such instruments as he thinks meete to make use of in this place....Know this is the place where the Lord will create a new Heaven, and a new Earth, in new Churches, and a new Common-wealth together.[10]

John Fiske, in *The Beginnings of New England,* called attention to the meticulous care of records and papers, done, not out of any sense of personal greatness, but with faith in the greatness of their undertaking, believed to be determinative of the future.

The colonies were not settled by individuals but by groups, in Massachusetts by *villages,* in Virginia as well as New England by *plantations,* which word has major reference to an ecclesiastical colony, and, in America, to a Christian colony, self-conscious of its status as such in the face of an alien world. This alien world good Christians saw as a potential empire under God. This emphasis with respect to colonies is apparent even in the "Instructions for the Councill appointed Forraigne Plantacons" by Charles II, 1660:

You are most especially to take an effectuall care of the propogacon of the Gospell in the severall Forraine Plantacons, by provideing that there be good encouragemt settled for the invitacon and maintenance of lerned and orthodox ministers, and by sending strict orders and injunccons for the regulating and reforming the debaucheries of planters and servants, whose ill example doth bring scandall upon Christianitie, and deterr such as yet are not admitted thereunto, from affecting or esteeming it. And you are to consider how such of the Natives or such as are purchased by you from other parts to be servants or slaves may be best invited to the Christian Faith, and be made capable of being baptized thereunto; it being the honor of our Crowne and of the Protestant Religion that all persons in any of our Dominions should be taught the knowledge of God, and be made acquainted with the misteries of Salvation.[11]

[10.] Hart, 366f. See Perry Miller, *Errand into the Wilderness* (Cambridge: Harvard University Press, 1956), 100: "I contend that the Virginia settlement, no less than the New England, lends itself to little more than a bare chronicle unless the cosmological and religious premises of the epoch are taken into account."

[11.] Hart, 186. Ostensible evidence to the contrary is Richard Eburne, *A Plain Pathway to Plantations* (1624), edited by Louis B. Wright (Ithaca, N.Y.: Cornell University Press, 1962). Eburne stressed economic gain as well as Christian goals. But for Eburne there was no conflict between the two. Economic gain of an honest sort was seen as thoroughly godly.

No cynicism was involved in this. It was assumed that, as surely as civil government was a necessity, so ecclesiastical government was a necessary condition of man's existence. The *forms* of church and state might be viewed with doubt, skepticism, or hostility, but the *idea* was assumed without question. Civil government was inescapably religious: the question was as to what form of religion was to be followed, and in what manner. The colonies, having their own charters and forms of government, saw themselves as Christian civil governments within the framework of the empire and under a common monarch. Rev. John Davenport, in *A Discourse about Civil Government in a New Plantation* (1674), declared that "the best Form of Government in a Christian Common-wealth, and which men that are free to chuse (as in new Plantations they are) ought to establish" is one in which they "make the Lord God our Governour."[12] It was thus assumed that a plantation was a new commonwealth in which men established their own Christian government under God. In every plantation, this assumption of the right to establish their own Christian society within the framework of the empire is to be found. The colonies were thus *holy commonwealths* planted in a new world on the basis of a faith in God and obedience to a covenant with God. The colonies might indeed have commercial goals in mind, but did not God promise to prosper His people? All the more because they sought human advantages and profits, it was necessary that they maintain the faith. As man kept that covenant, walking in faith and obedience, God in turn blessed him with His favor as a chosen instrument in history. In terms of this faith, Michael Wigglesworth (1631-1705), in *God's Controversy with New England* (1662), summoned the people to return to the covenant and fulfil their destiny as the holy commonwealth. As we have seen, three covenants were basic to this covenantal faith. First, the covenant of grace, a personal covenant, was inclusive of all redeemed men. It has reference to the fact of redemption and is thus inclusive of children as well as of adults. Man by grace is saved and made a covenant-keeper in Christ. This covenant is basic to all others, and to family, calling, ministry, magistracy, church, state, school, and every other human endeavor. Second, there is the church covenant, the church as the covenant people organized in terms of their churchly calling. Third, there is the civil covenant; Christian man creates a Christian civil government. This is not a confusion of church and state, but an insistent sense of obligation that the covenanted civil order, like every other order, fulfil its particular functions under God. The Christian state protects the church, and the church, by fulfilling its ministry, protects the state, but they are free from one another while coworkers under God. The Christian state thus had an obligation to maintain the sanctity of the oath, prohibit blasphemy, and further Christian law and order in the civil sphere, but it

---

[12.] Hart, 331.

could not become the church, nor govern the church, nor assume the church's responsibility. Thus, very early, we note an insistent pattern in the colonies, legislation designed to prohibit civil office to ministers, and even civil legislation against any magistrate serving a church as ruling elder while holding civil office.[13] Political rights did not depend on wealth nor on status, but upon a freeman's position with respect to the personal covenant of grace. If deemed a "visible saint," i.e., a mature and responsible Christian rather than a babe in Christ, he gained full membership and suffrage in the church, and also in the civil covenant.[14] In the early years of New England, political rights were more readily extended on the local village level than on the colonial level; later, the local level gained more power and became the stricter area with respect to suffrage. From the beginning, however, the local court was the most important one.

In New England, in the beginning, the church was not established; establishment and civil supremacy were indeed aspects of a common pattern against which the colonists were in varying degrees of rebellion. The establishment, when it came to Massachusetts, was a product of a mutual compromise designed to perpetuate the holy commonwealth rather than to return to the English pattern. The theological issues are not our present concern except in that, as the requirements for the mature fulfilment of the personal covenant moved from the Reformed doctrine of piety to Arminian moralism and experientialism, the people found themselves less able to share in the more private demands and tests of faith. Antinomianism had been the first manifestation of this demand for a private as against a public test. The compromise solution appeared in two ways. The church was established to create a *formally* Christian state and thereby retain the holy commonwealth goal. The church in turn established the world by means of the halfway covenant to ensure *formally* the coexistence of the church in the Christian Commonwealth. By his totally anarchistic and experiential test, Jonathan Edwards challenged not only the compromise but also the holy commonwealth idea, but failed. The attempt of Great Britain, in the years prior to the Revolution, to compel both civil and religious subservience to Parliament not only led to a rejection of parliamentary absolutism but of establishment in many areas. John Adams cited the attempt of Parliament to force the establishment of the Church of England on the colonies as responsible, "as much as any other cause," for the rethinking of constitutionalism which led to the challenge of parliamentary authority in general. "The objection was not

---

[13.] George Lee Haskins, *Law and Authority in Early Massachusetts* (New York: Macmillan, 1960), 249.
[14.] *Ibid.*, 103.

merely to the office of a bishop, though even that was dreaded, but to the authority of Parliament, on which it must be founded."[15]

The purpose of the New England colonies was, with respect to church and state, twofold: first, to establish the true and free church, free of the control of the state, free to be a coworker in terms of the Kingdom of God, to establish God's Zion on earth; second, to establish Godly magistrates, i.e., a Christian state, magistrates as ordained by God.

The English settlement, on the other hand, was well summarized by Hooker:

> We hold, that seeing there is not any man of the Church of England but the same man is also a member of the commonwealth; nor any man a member of the commonwealth which is not also of the Church of England; therefore as in a figure triangulare the base doth differ from the sides thereof, and yet one and the selfsame line is both a base and also a side; a side simply, a base if it chance to be the bottom and under lie the rest: so albeit properties and actions of one kind do cause the name of a commonwealth, qualities and functions of another sort the name of a Church to be given to a multitude, yet one and the selfsame multitude may in such sort be both, and is so with us that no person appertaining to the one can be denied to be also of the other....
>
> The Church and the commonwealth therefore are in this case personally one society, which society being termed a commonwealth as it liveth under whatsoever form of secular law and regiment, a church as it hath the spiritual law of Jesus Christ....[16]

This statement makes apparent the radical cleavage between the New England way and the English settlement. For Hooker, the two orders of church and state were truly one, reverse sides of a common coin at best. For New England, the goal was two free covenantal orders coinciding by means of the Christian faith of covenanted man. The coincidence thus was *not legal but spiritual*, resting on the personal covenant of grace. Establishment thus necessitated a halfway covenant; it was a rejection of legal coincidence while at the same time a recognition of a measure of Christian faith, concern, or interest on the part of it adherents. Since membership in the church covenant was not legal but spiritual, the issue was this: what constituted that spiritual membership? The Reformation position was that regeneration is the only ground of membership in the church invisible and in Jesus Christ, but that the visible church cannot know the heart. It must require therefore covenantal baptism, symbolical of the remission of sins, a faithful profession of faith, and a life lived, however frail, sinful, and faulty, in terms of conformity to that profession. The pressure in New England

---

[15.] John Adams, *Works*, vol. X (Boston: Little, Brown, 1865), 185, letter to Dr. J. Morse, 2 December 1815. Adams' statement has been confirmed by Carl Bridenbaugh's able study, *Mitre and Sceptre*.
[16.] Richard Hooker, *Laws of Ecclesiastical Polity*, Book VIII, i, 2, 4

from Quakers, antinomians and Anabaptists was to demand a knowledge of a surer sort concerning the validity of profession, and Edwards represented the same demand. New England preferred, as it faced these early threats, to risk hypocrisy as against an implicit claim to omniscience. Its problem was thus one which could not exist in the legal status of church membership in England, where ecclesiastical courts could govern acts and words (heresy), having a valid negative jurisdiction, but could not positively assert the church's own free existence. As against this English settlement, Thomas Cartwright early asserted the Reformed doctrine:

> For justice may be as well accused for wrong doing, as this doctrine for bringing in disorder, whose whole work is to provide that nothing be done out of place, out of time, or otherwise than the condition of every man's calling will bear; which putteth the people in subjection under their governors, the governors in degree and order one under another, as the elder under the pastor, and the deacon under the elder; which teacheth that a particular church shall give place unto a provincial synod, where many churches are, and the provincial to a national, and likewise that unto the general, if any be, and all unto Christ and his word. When, on the contrary part, those which stand against this doctrine are thereby compelled to bring into the church great confusion and marvellous disorder, whilst the pastor's office is confounded with the deacon's; whilst women do minister the sacraments, which is lawful only for men; whilst private men do that which belongeth unto public persons; while public actions are done in private places; whilst the church is shuffled with the commonwealth; whilst civil matters are handled by ecclesiastical persons, and ecclesiastical by those which be civil....[17]

This was, of course, a demand for the freedom of the church. Whether Separatist or non-Separatist, New England Puritans were dedicated to this doctrine, a dedication later common to men in all the colonies. Their conception of society was in terms of the holy commonwealth idea, resting on the threefold covenant. Richard Baxter's *A Holy Commonwealth* (1659) was widely read in New England, as was another work, by John Eliot of Roxbury, Massachusetts, *Christian Commonwealth: or, The Civil Polity of the Rising Kingdom of Jesus Christ* (1660). The forms proposed by these men did not remain, but the concept was common to New England, and increasingly to the other colonies. New England provided the intellectual leadership for America, and its eminence was very real. As Middleton has commented, in another context, "It is interesting to note that, except in the political realm, Virginia's culture was largely absorptive rather than productive. In this way it differed from the culture of New England where Cotton Mather could publish no fewer than 450 books and pamphlets in a

---

[17.] Thomas Cartwright, "Epistle to the Church of England," cited from Archbishop Whitgift, *Works*, vol. I (Cambridge, Mass.: Parker Society, 1851), 18.

single lifetime."[18] In New England, as well as elsewhere, there was a lack of interest in missionary work because it was felt that priority should be given to their central concern, the holy commonwealth, of which every man's progress and prosperity was a basic part. Their great historical task was summed up in that concept. "The idea of the Holy Commonwealth made it easy for the Puritans to bring their philosophy of history up to date. God was evidently merely completing the work which he began in the Reformation."[19] Wyclif had reestablished man's prophetic office, Luther his priestly office, and now, with guidance from Calvin, New England would establish man's kingly office, and Christ would thus reign in his saints of New England.

The history of the holy commonwealth idea has been treated from another perspective by H. Richard Niebuhr in *The Kingdom of God in America* (1937). First, in the colonial era, the sovereignty of God was the dominant idea, with a reordering of church, state, and society in terms of His infallible word. Second, the emphasis was shifted from the transcendent and triune God to the incarnate Christ and the reign of Christ, an emphasis on the relational rather than ontological aspect of God the Son. This era was marked by the rise of Arminianism, revivalism, crusades of reform in the nineteenth century, early Unitarianism, and other movements. Third, the social gospel arose to stress the Kingdom of God on earth in America. The emphasis is on earth and America, and the dynamic is human impulse rather than the sovereignty of God. Statist legislation becomes the means to establishing the Kingdom.

The Puritan conception of law and liberty differed markedly from the modern view. Since Christ is both life and liberty, *the beginning of liberty is the discipline of Christ. His* word, Scripture, is the means to freedom in every area of life, in that *liberty is under law,* and is not, as in the modern view, liberty *from* law. The freedom from law bestowed by Christ is not antinomian; it is freedom from damnation by the law into power to live by a new nature in *the law as liberty.* The Christian view *requires* discipline and discipleship; the second *requires* freedom from discipline and restraint. The Puritans recognized that true discipline is self-discipline, and is therefore an inner rather than an outer compulsion. Outer compulsion should do no more than establish conditions for the development of inner compulsion. But how produced? In *A Remonstrance of Fairfax and the Council of Officers,* 16th November, 1648, Parliament was informed that their common struggle had been to establish "common right and freedom," but, since true religion alone makes men free, and Godlessness and superstition are alike

---

18. Arthur Pierce Middleton, *A Virginia Gentleman's Library, as proposed by Thomas Jefferson to Robert Skipwith in 1771* (Virginia: Colonial Williamsburg, 1959), 6. The political thought, of course, did not come until the era of the break with Britain.
19. Herbert Wallace Schneider, *The Puritan Mind* (Ann Arbor: University of Michigan Ann Arbor Paperbacks, 1958), 27f.

allies of the tyrant,[20] it was necessary to give freedom to the church, dissolve the establishment, and work for a Christian order in the state. Earlier, the martyrs Barrow and Greenwood held strongly to the same faith. Greenwood had said, of the English settlement and of all such unions of civil and ecclesiastical offices, "This mixture is the mystery of iniquity and the power of the beast."[21]

Two emphases are here to be noted. First, it was held that *church and state are separate in office without separation of faith.* This was the meaning of "separation" in the American tradition, with rare exceptions. It was assumed that the state *must* be Christian, but it is today denied, in terms of the doctrine of separation, that the state has any *right* to be Christian. Second, liberty is a Christian order of life, and liberty rests in God *under law.* Sir Walter Scott, in writing a "War Song of the Royal Edinburgh Light Dragoons" (1797), expressed his own opposition to the French Revolution and its antinomian concept of liberty by means of this faith:

> To horse! to horse! the sabres gleam;
> High sounds our bugle-call;
> Combined by honour's sacred tie,
> Our word is Laws and Liberty!
> March forward, one and all!

Notice the reference to *laws* rather than to *law* by Scott. This particularity was a characteristic of feudalism, English law, of Biblical law, and developed in Puritanism. The particularity of the American Revolution (which marked it rather as a Rebellion), as against the abstractness of French revolutionary concepts, was noted by Tocqueville, and has been stressed by Boorstin.[22]

The religious delight in *law as liberty* was well expressed by a New England minister and poet, Edward Taylor (d. 1729), who wrote:

> Oh! What a thing is Man? Lord, who am I?
> That thou shouldest give him Law (Oh! Golden Line)
> To regulate his Thoughts, Words, Life thereby.[23]

To Godly man, law is not an enemy but his mainstay. Hence, the religious delight these men felt in law, and, supremely, in God's law. The study of Biblical doctrine was thus an exercise in liberty, so that John Cotton could say, "I love to sweeten my mouth with a piece of *Calvin,* before I go to sleep."[24] The severe Puritan laws, therefore, represented the social

---

[20.] A. S. P. Woodhouse, ed., *Puritanism and Liberty* (London: Dent, 1938), 64, 458f.

[21.] F. J. Powicke, *Henry Barrow, Separatist, and the Exiled Church of Amsterdam, 1593-1622* (London: Clark, 1900), 50.

[22.] Daniel J. Boorstin, *The Genius of American Politics* (Chicago: University of Chicago Press, 1953), 82f.

[23.] Thomas H. Johnson, ed., *The Poetical Works of Edward Taylor* (Princeton, N.J.: Princeton University Press, 1943), 146. On Taylor, see also Norman S. Grabo, ed., *Christographia* (New Haven: Yale University Press, 1962).

[24.] Johnson, 19.

expression of love for men. The laws respecting children, as an example, were severe,[25] and yet, as one critic has admitted, the Puritans were so devoted to their children that "in general they would suffer crucifixion" for them.[26] At the same time, love meant law and discipline. Hence, in many poor dwellings, where there were only two chairs or a bench, the parents sat to eat and the children stood at the table.

Liberty was law, and both concepts were Biblical, not rationalistic. Law and power were both transcendental concepts; hence their separation in the sphere of government, to prevent an immanent collection of transcendental attributes. In the American tradition, rationalism meant both reductionism, a radical impoverishment, and an attempt to play God. The issue was sharply joined in John Adams' marginal note on a sentence by Mary Wollstonecraft:

> M. W.: Who *will* dare to assert that obedience to parents should go one jot beyond the deference due to reason, enforced by affection?
>
> A.: Would you make the child the judge?[27]

The theological inheritance of Puritanism made it hostile both to the rationalistic approach and, in the period prior to the early nineteenth century, to the emotional approach. Both involved a reductionism and a dissolution of the holy commonwealth in favor of (subjective) judgment or experience. As Woodhouse has noted, every attempt in England and America to establish a holy commonwealth is an instance of a form of Calvinism or of Puritanism, and every departure from this concept is a departure from Puritanism and Calvinism.[28] The departures were antinomian and gnostic as well, in that they assumed a private or subjective experience and possession of truth. Ann Hutchinson, for example, in three years' time brought no small chaos to Massachusetts by holding that the Puritan standard, which did not claim a heart-knowledge as the necessary test of faith, was "a covenant of works" because it limited itself to the facts of an outward profession of faith and a life lived in conformity to it. She was charged by the deputy governor, according to Thomas Hutchinson's *History of the Province of Massachusetts-Bay* (1768), with declaring further "that those under a covenant of works could not be saved." Although she challenged them to "prove that I said so," the logic of her position left her no other conclusion. Salvation is in the covenant of grace, but, if the church or men rather than God is the judge of that grace, then an omniscience is

---

25. *The Code of 1650 of the General Court of Connecticut* (Hartford, Ct.: Andrus, 1822), 29f.

26. Dana Doten, *The Art of Bundling* (New York: Farrar and Rinehart, 1938), 58.

27. Zolton Haraszti, *John Adams and the Prophets of Progress* (Cambridge, Mass.: Harvard University Press, 1952), 193.

28. Woodhouse, 36.

claimed, a knowledge of the heart impossible to men. The Puritan position was that a tree was to be judged by its fruits, and faith by its works. Experimentalism and rationalism were thus two forms of gnosticism and reductionism which were to challenge insistently the holy commonwealth idea. Rationalism found its strongest expression in the French Revolution and the Jacobin Clubs, and experientialism in nineteenth century revivalism and Romanticism.

The problem to Massachusetts, which colony was a standing and central offense to antinomians and gnostics, was the insistence of these people in invading her frontiers to protest the Massachusetts way. Quaker women, especially given to extravagant protests, such as going naked publicly to "reveal" symbolically the "nakedness" of Massachusetts' religion, were an embarrassing problem. The solution with all such fanatics, of which Roger Williams was one (his religious toleration later is used to excuse his predominantly unstable stands), was to oust them. The land was open for them to move on and establish their own colonies. Executions in a few cases followed persistent returns to Massachusetts in efforts to subvert the state order. Many of the offending persons were clearly psychotic, a fact which does not eliminate their responsibility. As Hildreth has observed:

> There was this peculiarity, indeed, in all the New England persecutions, with the single exception of Gorton's case, that heretics were persecuted, not so much as enemies of God, whom it was fit and meretorious to punish, but rather as intruders, whom it was desirable to get rid of, or at least to silence.[29]

The right to emigration existed. The Indian population was negligible in New England before the first successful settlement because of various major epidemics among the Indians. New England was to be free to pursue and develop its particular faith in a holy commonwealth. To this it gave intelligent and educated attention. In Massachusetts especially, the men were persons of wealth, ability, and education, with a high ratio of university men.[30] Massachusetts was one of the best markets for books anywhere, and as early as 1677, there were four booksellers in little Boston, and Usher, its richest merchant, had acquired his fortune through bookselling.[31] The holy commonwealth idea furthered education, emphasized character, and created a new conception of man and society. Note the tribute of a hostile witness:

[29.] Richard Hildreth, *The History of the United States*, vol. I, rev. ed. (New York: Harper, 1882), 408. Church censure, according to the Puritans, had to be exercised in most cases with patience and was "slow and gradual"; see *A Brief Narration of the Practices of the Churches in New England* (London, 1645).

[30.] Haskins, *Law and Authority in Early Massachusetts*, 12, 235.

[31.] Hildreth, 497.

> Even the theocratic form of government prevailing in New England
> tended to diminish the influence of wealth, by introducing a different
> basis of distinction; and still more so that activity of mind, the
> consequence of strong religious excitement, developing constantly
> new views of religion and politics, which an arrogant and supercilious
> theocracy strove in vain to suppress. Hence, in New England a
> constant tendency toward social equality.[32]

The meaning is clear: neither wealth, nor caste, nor blood was important,
but Christian character. The older concepts of status were thus bypassed in
favor of one which made possible the sturdy character and strong sense of
communion which non-religious scholars have termed New England
democracy.

The holy commonwealth was a theocracy in that it rested on the
sovereignty of God and His kingship. With respect to the human order, it
was a commonwealth. There was no rule of the state by the church, or vice
versa. The church, according to the Westminster Confession, was to be
ready for consultation with the state when a point with reference to the
Biblical standard was desired, and had the right to speak in cases
extraordinary, but it was otherwise limited to its own realm. The new
charter for Massachusetts in 1692 was regarded a downward step, and
marked a formal order of execution for the holy commonwealth in that
colony, but it failed to die.

The holy commonwealth, while resting on the personal covenant of
grace, refused to be reduced to the individual experience of grace or to more
than a formal test of it. When Saltonstall pleaded with Massachusetts
against intolerance of dissenters, the leaders affirmed a readiness to risk
fostering hypocrisy in order to maintain "God's institutions" and "unity in
the foundation of religion and church order." They denied seeking
"uniformity;" the integrity of the holy commonwealth idea was rather
their objective.[33]

The decline and defeat of the Great Awakening is sometimes seen as the
end of the commonwealth idea. In actuality, the defeat of the Great
Awakening, fought in pulpit, village square, court, and in state actions, was
a triumph of the holy commonwealth. As Schneider clearly saw, "Edwards
was surprisingly blind to the political philosophy of the Holy
Commonwealth. Though he was preoccupied with a History of
Redemption (published in 1739).... he nowhere mentions it."[34] The "Jewish

---

[32.] *Ibid.*, 510.

[33.] Hildreth, 383-5. In an early Puritan confession of faith, dated from Newgate, December 4, 1572, it was declared, "We are not for an unspotted Church on earth" but for *reformation*, which does not mean *perfection*. In terms of this, the "Puritans" a little later protested against being "christened with the odious name of Puritans," Daniel Neal, *History of the Puritans*, vol. I (New York: Harper, 1844), 122, 153.

commonwealth" is mentioned in passing, and the Christian common-wealth is often close to the surface but never in clear perspective. Edwards' perspective was psychological, and the universe was reduced to the soul and experience of man. Platonism and Locke had taken their toll in his thinking, and he wanted to substitute for the holy commonwealth the religious experience of the individual. Religious experience had its place in the commonwealth, but, as mastered in Edwards, it tolerated nothing else. Entrance into the church was conditional upon experience with Edwards, not upon the covenant. Covenant, commonwealth, and all else were dissolved by this preeminence of psychology. Edwards destroyed sphere law and the validity of Christian man as priest, prophet, and king in each area. *The essence of Christianity was now the religious experience. Man was religious man only when possessed by the religious sentiment or affections. Edwards did not see, as Calvin did, man as always religious man, whether covenant-keeper or covenant-breaker. Edwards' man was Enlightenment man, basically secular except when possessed by religious experience.* Religious experience thus became frenzy, and an addition to nature. Much of the opposition to Edwards has been called "liberalism"; it was not. Commonwealth thinking, whether strictly or loosely Calvinistic, did unite against Edwards, and their areas of agreement were substantial, and what was called, then and earlier, "liberal" was at times no more than a rejection of experientialism. Thus, Boston's new church was organized in 1698 and Benjamin Colman invited as pastor. The new church pledged itself to the Westminster Confession and declared that "we assume not to ourselves to impose upon any a public relation of their experiences." Colman had received a Presbyterian ordination and represented, as Cotton Mather recognized, a contradiction to his own experiential tendencies. In his *Diary*, Mather admitted that the new group claimed "that they would not vary from the Practice of these Churches, except in one little Particular."[35]

Edwardianism succeeded in one respect, in that it deepened the cleavage in the church. By its demand for experientialism, it placed other churches in disrepute as dens of iniquity and hypocrisy. Puritanism and the limited religious liberalism of the day had to champion the cause of the

[34.] Schneider, *The Puritan Mind*, 106. For a report, analysis, and a very able assessment of some of the positive results of the Great Awakening, see C. C. Goen, *Revivalism and Separatism in New England, 1740-1800* (New Haven, Ct.: Yale University Press, 1962). Goen gives evidence of the antinomianism, chiliasm, and perfectionism in the Great Awakening (200ff.), which included in some instances a forsaking of marriage and a belief in immediate perfection and immortality. The major thrust of the movement, however, was, according to Goen, its development of a new impetus in Christian faith and its major contribution to disestablishment.
[35.] *Diary of Cotton Mather*, vol. 1, 1681-1709 (New York: Ungar, n.d), 326. Of Colman, Perry Miller states that he "was never to exhibit the slightest sign of being anything but a faithful Calvinist," *The New England Mind, From Colony to Province*, (Cambridge, Mass.: Harvard University Press, 1962), 242.

commonwealth without being able to assert the church's unwavering and unified role therein. The result became apparent in colonial election sermons, which shifted from an attempt to preserve the integrity of the *church* to an attempt to preserve the integrity of civil government.[36] The holy commonwealth was now increasingly civil *government and Christianity* rather than church and state, or civil and ecclesiastical governments. Thus, while the Great Awakening was defeated by 1660, and the holy commonwealth faith triumphant, it was with marked changes. Furthermore, the bitter resentment against the enforced establishments by Parliament worked at the same time to further the concept of pluralistic church governments, or at least establishments, so that Christianity rather than a particular church group represented the faith of Christian civil government. Christianity rather than a particular church was thus the "establishment."

In this form, the holy commonwealth idea remained central to American life. Unitarianism itself represented a humanistic variation of this faith, with the state schools as the new church and partner to the state. Other groups saw the state schools as Protestant establishments (and Roman Catholics feared them as such), and the Bible found its place in the schoolroom. Revivalism, while experiential, was likewise concerned with the holy commonwealth. Its experientialism dissolved the church but not Christian civil government. Revivalism was undenominational and very often anti-denominational. It was not greatly concerned with reviving the church, in many instances, but rather with reviving America. Its cry was, "Save America." Hence its interdenominationalism and intense patriotism. Hence also the fact that civil dignitaries quickly developed close connections with revivals and appeared on platforms. Thus today Billy Graham is ready to work with all churches, and have dignitaries of state on the platform with him, because it is a Godly and revived America, not a particular church, which is his human focus. However much denounced by church bodies, he is closer to civil authorities than are highly organized religious bodies because his ministry is national, not ecclesiastical. This approach is a development of the nineteenth century and not to be confused with the theocentric colonial view of the holy commonwealth. A Roman Catholic comment is to the point: "the role of the churches in America is not to save America. The day they make that their purpose, they have failed as churches."[37] The holy commonwealth idea today is anthropocentric in its theology, unfortunately, rather than theocentric.

---

[36]. See Edward Frank Humphrey, *Nationalism and Religion in America, 1774-1789* (Boston: Chipman Publishing Co., 1924).
[37]. Gustave Weigel, S.J., *Faith and Understanding in America* (New York: Macmillan, 1962), 64.

Cotton Mather himself, while sharing with Edwards both an experiential and rationalistic reductionism, nonetheless held to an alliance of civil government and Christianity. Mather's best disciple in many respects was Benjamin Franklin, who, despite extensive dabbling in every kind of thought, and despite his ridicule of Mather on one occasion, not only paid his respects to Mather but also remained a faithful follower of Mather's *Essays to do Good*. Franklin's "honesty is the best policy" is Mather's doctrine, i.e., that Christian faith and morality are the soundest policies for national and personal health. Cotton Mather saw Christianity as both religion and virtue to a state in this form; he felt that Christian America had a great destiny:

> The works of our day I take to be as follows:
>
> 1. The revivals of primitive christianity: to endeavor to restore every thing of the primitive character. The apostacy is going off. The time for cleansing the temple comes on. More EDWARDS would be vast blessings, when the primitive doctrines of christianity are corrupted.
>
> 2. The persuading of the European powers to shake off the chains of popery. Let this argument be used; there is no popish nation but would, by embracing the protestant religion, not only introduce itself into a glorious liberty, but also would double its wealth immediately. It *is* strange, that this has not been more attended to. Let it be prosecuted with more demonstration. A certain writer has shown, that the abolition of popery in England is worth at least eight millions sterling to the nation, annually. Let this argument arising from interest, be tried with other nations.
>
> 3. The formation and quickening of the people who are to be "the stone out of the mountain." In this thing, as in some others, "none of the wicked shall understand; but the wise shall understand." God will do his own work in his own time and manner; and Austin says, "it is advisable to withhold part of what I meant to say, because of men's incapacity to receive it."[38]

Mather, in spite of his support of Edwards, was attacked by James Davenport, an itinerant preacher of the Great Awakening, as a worldly preacher. At New London, Connecticut, Davenport directed his converts to bring in books by Cotton Mather, Benjamin Colman, and others for burning.

With the failure of the Great Awakening, the ecclesiastical concern became less prominent. Any and all forms of establishment were increasingly opposed on religious grounds. The Constitution very nearly failed to secure ratification because of the hostility of Protestant clergymen

---

[38.] Cotton Mather, *Essays to do Good* (Wilmington, Del.: George Burder edition, 1822), 185f. Benjamin Franklin, in a letter, wrote of Mather's *Essays to do Good*, "If I have been…a useful citizen, the public owes the advantage of it to that book," Ralph Barton Perry, *Puritanism and Democracy* (New York: Vanguard, 1944), 324.

to the possibility of establishment. It became necessary to ensure the federal union against establishment to satisfy *the churches*.[39] The move for the First Amendment, and note its priority, was not *an instance of secularism but of religious convictions*. Its purpose was "freedom of religion *for* religion," not "freedom *from* religion."[40]

So strong was the feeling with respect to freeing both church and civil government from interference from one another, that many states limited the right of clergy to civil office at the same time as they barred the civil government from establishing or governing the church. Ezra Stiles declared in 1783, that, while indifference of people and civil government to Christianity was to be feared, God was to be thanked for the restraint placed upon confusion of the two orders, "for I wish the clergy never to be vested with civil power."[41] This feeling was widespread and common to the orthodox clergy and to civil officers. Thus, Georgia barred ministers from serving in the state legislature but at the same time limited admission to the legislature to Protestants only.[42] It saw itself thus as a Protestant and Christian state, preserving the freedom of both church and state. Its Protestantism was, however, "American" and equally hostile to European Protestant and Catholic establishments. New York barred ministers or priests from all civil or military office in the state,[43] and similar legislation was enacted in North Carolina, Virginia, South Carolina, Kentucky, Tennessee, and Louisiana.[44] Test oaths, blasphemy laws, and other legislation reinforced the idea that *the particular states intended to be Christian states, but not ecclesiastically oriented states*. Although the Massachusetts Bill of Rights specified that no one should be molested for his religious profession, this was not construed as permitting assault on the Christian nature of the state, and, in the 1840s, the blasphemy law was upheld by the state supreme court. A law enacted in 1649 imposing a fine, then whipping, then banishment, then death, to "any who denied the received books of the Old and New Testaments to be the infallible word of God,"[45] remained on the books together with the blasphemy law. Much of such legislation is still on the statute books across the country and is sometimes cited as "relics" of church control. Rather than church control, these laws testify to the concept of the Christian Commonwealth. Sabbath

---

[39.] Robert Allen Rutland, *The Birth of the Bill of Rights, 1776-1791* (Chapel Hill: University of North Carolina Press), 127f., 151, 166.

[40.] See Joseph J. Costonzo, S.J., "Religion in Public School Education," *Thought*, Fordham University Quarterly, 31, no. 121, Summer, 1956.

[41.] Thornton, *Pulpit of the American Revolution*, 488.

[42.] Rutland, 61.

[43.] *Ibid.*, 63.

[44.] Tocqueville, vol. I, 337.

[45.] Hildreth, 369f.

laws were a commonplace evidence of this same fact. The Constitution (Article I, Section 7) made a point of exempting Sundays as legally countable days with reference to the presidential veto. Chancellor Kent, Justice Story, and others emphasized the non-sectarian and Christian character of the federal union. Virtually every state constitution placed itself under God in some form, as witness the preamble to the California Constitution: "We the people of the State of California grateful to Almighty God for our freedom, in order to secure and perpetuate its blessings, do establish this Constitution." But the presence or absence of such references is peripheral. Civil government was assumed to be, on every level, a Christian order, but not an ecclesiastical institution. The idea of a secular state came into focus only with the French Revolution and was an alien concept to the United States. The insistence on the Christian commonwealth idea was especially tenacious in New Hampshire, which only in 1902 changed the word "Protestant" in its Bill of Rights to "Christian," and refused in 1912 to eliminate it. From the English background, Christianity had a common law status in the United States,[46] but it also had a status, not as a religious institution or society, but as the nature of the government. The Supreme Court in the Trinity Church Case, 1892, found in "American life...its laws... customs... everywhere a clear recognition of the same truth. These add a volume of unofficial declarations to the mass of organic utterances that this is a Christian nation." As a part of this same temper, as recently as 1952, Congress enacted legislation calling upon the president to proclaim a National Day of Prayer, and in 1954 added the words "under God" to the Pledge of Allegiance. The National Anthem gives witness to a like faith, and even recent Supreme Court decisions, despite the New York school prayer case of 1962, have acknowledged some aspect or another of this inheritance. A poll subsequent to the school prayer case showed eighty percent approving religious observances in schools and only fourteen percent opposing them. Another poll showed an even higher percent favoring some kind of

[46.] For an example of such legal use of the Bible, see a New Hampshire divorce case decision, 1836, given in Jacob W. Ehrlich, *The Holy Bible and the Law* (New York: Oceana, 1962), 66-79. In England, Blackstone had cited the fact that "blasphemy against the Almighty, by denying His being or providence; or by contumelious reproaches of our Saviour Christ....these are offenses punishable at common law...; for Christianity *is* part of the *law* of England" (Bk IV, c.4. s.iv). This was borne out by English courts until 1917, when the House of Lords decision of *Bowman v. Secular Society* set aside this concept as "rhetoric" despite its fully legal use earlier; see Lord Radcliffe, *The Law and Its Compass* (Evanston, Ill.: Northwestern University Press, 1960), 16-22. Newman, on his notification of the cardinalate, declared that, "unless the Almighty interferes," the end of the nineteenth century would see the end of the fact of Christianity as the law of the land in England and in other Christian countries. The reason for this decline was "Liberalism in religion"; James Collins, ed., *Philosophical Readings in Cardinal Newman* (Chicago: Regnery, 1961), 3343f.

religious test for teachers. As against both popular and federal positions, Herman Hoeksema, a Calvinist theologian, asserted a position more understandable to the founding fathers:

> Our standpoint is that the education of our children is not the obligation of the government, but of parents....It must be emphasized that the education in the schools is not the business of the State or of the government, but of the parents.
>
> This is the principle reason why I dissent from either the majority or the minority opinion of the Supreme Court of the United States.[47]

Jefferson was a militant foe of statist education. "He was opposed to state subsidies for local government functions....Rather than have a system of schools managed for rather than by the people, Jefferson would have withdrawn his support of the proposed system entirely. As well, he thought, commit the management of farms, mills, and stores to the government and council."[48]

This stand was but one facet of the doctrine of the priesthood of all believers, and the concept of sphere laws and their transcendental unity in God. This was held to be Protestantism, and monopoly and centralization was monarchy and Romanism. Thus, Shelburne, speaking to Parliament on the question of the colonial rebellion, said, on February 17, 1783:

> Monopolies, some way or other, are ever justly punished. They forbid rivalry, and rivalry is the very essence of the well-being of trade. This seems to be the era of protestantism in trade. All Europe appears enlightened and eager to throw off the vile shackles of oppressive, ignorant, unmanly monopoly.[49]

The extent to which this logic was carried is too seldom appreciated. Disestablishment was a concept applied not only to the church but also to man's economic and other activities. Thus, in Rhode Island, just after the Revolution, state construction of a turnpike road across that state was blocked on these grounds and was not overcome until 1805:

> ...turnpikes and the establishment of religious worship had their origin in Great Britain, the government of which was a monarchy and the inhabitants slaves;...the people of Massachusetts and Connecticut were obliged by law to support ministers and pay the fare of turnpikes, and were therefore slaves also; that if they chose to be slaves they undoubtedly had a right to their choice; but the free-born Rhode Islanders ought never to submit to be priest-ridden, nor to pay for the privilege of travelling on the highway.[50]

47. Herman Hoeksema, "As to Prayer in Public Schools," *The Standard Bearer*, 38, no. 21, (5 September 1962, Grand Rapids, Mich.), 504, 584.
48. Charles H. Ambler, *A History of Education in West Virginia, from Early Colonial Times to 1949* (Huntington, W. Va: Standard, 1951), 19f.
49. George Bancroft, *History of the Formation of the Constitution of the United States of America*, vol. 1 (New York: Appleton, 1882), 52.

In 1776, the population of the United States was approximately three million, of which 20,000 were Roman Catholics, with Jews, as late as 1790, numbering only 1,243. The 20,000 Catholics included women, children, and slaves. Of these, the men were thus a limited number. Some fought for the English, holding the Revolution to be a "Presbyterian war," but many fought with honor for the American cause.[51]

While the majority of the U. S. population were definitely not church members in the modern sense, it should be recalled that nonmembership did not mean a separation from the church but could and commonly did accompany lifelong and faithful attendance. The general population very definitely saw itself as Protestant and Christian and believed in the freedom of both civil and ecclesiastical governments as Christian orders. This "Protestantism" was not European Protestantism but closer to anti-clericalism, and was generally shared by clergy and laity. Again, it was not European anti-clericalism, but rather a belief that neither ecclesiastical nor civil government could legitimately claim the right to dominate the other. Many New England Congregationalists were less in accord with this view than were Roman Catholics at this period. Catholics, for whom the ideas of a Christian republic, the denial of human and institutional sovereignty, and coordinate relationship of church and state had deep roots, were ready to challenge many developments in their communion in the name of the Catholic faith. That they were influenced by America is clearcut, but the reduction of their position to "Americanism" is a serious injustice.

For an understanding of the relationship of civil government and Christianity, it is important to understand that the older view was markedly different from the modern, simplistic view. The issues were well stated in the Whitehall Debates, 1648, of Cromwell's army, and they are fundamental to an understanding of much future Puritan and American thought. This developed position can be summed up in four points:

1. It was believed increasingly that the state should have no power in the government of the church or churches. Such power constituted an unbiblical confusion.

2. This by no means meant that there would be no relationship between Christianity and civil government. It was assumed that the civil order would be a Christian commonwealth.

3. The question therefore was this: was the magistrate's relationship to matters of religion *compulsive* or *restrictive?* To be compulsive meant to

---

[50.] Cited from Timothy Dwight in Henry Adams, *The United States in 1800* (Ithaca, N.Y.: Cornell Great Seal Books, 1955), 45.
[51.] See Charles H. Metzger, S.J., *Catholics and the American Revolution* (Chicago: Loyola, 1962). Metzger's excellent study calls attention to the Protestant climate of the Revolution, and the reasons for Catholic support thereof.

require a particular kind of theology, govern church attendance, and the like. To be restrictive meant to preserve the state or civil order from erosion by barring immoral and profligate men, unbelievers, and criminals from civil office and suffrage. It meant the exclusion of practices odious to Christian faith, i.e., abortion, polygamy, cannibalism, and the like.

4. Without some restrictive right of religion, a state was not believed to be possible. Law is the expression of a doctrine of morality and of justice, and hence a civil government inevitably presupposes an ethic, which in itself is the expression of a metaphysic. Religion in at least a restrictive sense is hence unavoidable for civil government. To deny that relativism or humanism is a religion, ethic, or metaphysic, does not make it any the less so. The Supreme Court of the United States is in process of disestablishing Christianity as the restrictive basis of civil order and in process of establishing relativism. The present constitutional crisis is centered on this fact: the Court is in process of effecting a transition from the United States as a Christian Commonwealth to the establishment of relativism and a unitary and absolute state, John Dewey's "democratic" Great Community. In consequence of this change, *procedural* due process has triumphed over *substantive* due process with reference to courtroom practice.[52] The developing substantive element is *total democracy*.

The first challenge to the American system came with the French Revolution. No understanding of the administrations of Washington and Adams is possible apart from this context. The Alien Act and the Alien Enemies Act were designed to protect the United States from the extensive French Jacobin conspiracy, paid agents of which were even in high places in the government. The Alien Act was not enforced, since two or three shiploads of such French aliens promptly left the country. The Sedition Act led to ten convictions on political grounds and was soon repealed. Washington's concern was not only with the military dangers inherent in a foreign entanglement, but also the religious and philosophical issues involved. In his Farewell Address, September 17, 1796, Washington, keenly mindful of the groups of American sympathizers to the French Revolution and adherents of that current of thought, spoke to that issue. He questioned the validity of what is now termed a secular state. With an eye on what had transpired in France, the open assault, as Burke in 1791 declared, on the idea of a Christian state, Washington said:

> Of all the dispositions and habits, which lead to political prosperity, religion and morality are indispensable supports. In vain would that man claim the tribute of patriotism, who should labor to subvert these

---

[52.] See Francis H. Heller, *The Sixth Amendment to the Constitution of the United States, A Study in Constitutional Development* (Lawrence, Kans.: University of Kansas Press, 1951), 90ff., 147ff.

great pillars of human happiness, these firmest props of the duties of men and citizens. The mere politician, equally with the pious man, ought to respect, and to cherish them. A volume could not trace all their connexions with private and public felicity. Let it simply be asked, Where is the security for property, for reputation, for life, if the sense of religious obligation deserts the oaths, which are the instruments of investigation in courts of justice? And let us with caution indulge the supposition, that morality can be maintained without religion. Whatever may be conceded to the influence of refined education on minds of peculiar structure, reason and experience both forbid us to expect, that national morality can prevail in exclusion of religious principle.

It is substantially true, that virtue or morality is a necessary spring of every popular government. The rule, indeed, extends with more or less force to every species of free government. Who, that is a sincere friend to it, can look with indifference upon attempts to shake the foundation the fabric? Promote, then, as an object of primary importance, institutions for the general diffusion of knowledge. In proportion as the structure of a government gives force to public opinion, it is essential that public opinion should be enlightened.[53]

But Washington's answer was not statist education, which did not then exist, but free Christian schools, the prevailing pattern of the day. These schools provided the world's most effective and extensive education in that day. A French observer in 1800 commented on the high calibre of public intelligence and understanding, which was a product of these schools.[54] The Northwest Ordinance of July 13, 1787, passed by the Confederation Congress, is important not only in that it contained the first federal bill of rights, but also in that it clearly favored the furtherance of Christian schools so that Christian civil government might be strengthened. According to Article III, "Religion, morality, and knowledge being necessary to good government and the happiness of mankind, schools and the means of education shall forever be encouraged." Schools were thus assumed to be the channels of religion and morality as well as of knowledge. Education was not statist: it was local and Christian, and it was the foundation of Christian civil society. The importance of the Northwest Ordinance has not been generally recognized, and is lost on the Supreme Court as well, in that after the passing of the First Amendment, this act of the Federation Congress was reenacted by the First Federal Congress. In this way it became clear that disestablishment did not mean the separation of Christianity from the Federal Union, nor the inability of Congress to further Christian government and culture. Divine worship was a part of Washington's inauguration and was held upon the order of Congress by the

[53.] Richardson, 220.
[54.] Du Pont de Nemours, *National Education in the United States of America*, translated from the second French edition of 1812 and with an Introduction by B. G. du Pont (Newark: University of Delaware Press, 1923), 3ff.

Chaplain of Congress. The radical, Joel Barlow (1754-1812), as U. S. consul in Algiers, asserted in Article XI of the treaty with Tripoli of February 10, 1797, a statement that the United States "is not, in any sense, founded on the Christian religion," but the Treaty of Peace and Amity signed in Tripoli, June 4, 1805, struck out that clause in "virtual repudiation of the negative statement in the original treaty," an act all the more significant in that it came during Jefferson's administration.[55] Although Jefferson was closer to the radical Barlow than other presidents, worship was held in Congress during his administration, with Roman Catholic, Quaker, and Unitarian clergymen included, as well as Orthodox Protestants. These were activities assumed to be right and necessary; they were the American way. As against the menace of Jacobin doctrine, with reference both to foreign policy and to religious principles, Washington said, "Why quit our own to stand upon foreign ground?"[56] The isolation espoused by Washington was political, philosophical, and religious. It was bent on keeping the peace militarily and on preserving the American historical tradition in its separateness and integrity.

Tocqueville noted the strongly Christian nature of the young republic. "In the United States of America the sovereign authority is religious."[57] He cited evidences of this, in particular the refusal to accept the testimony of an atheist. Thus, in Chester County, New York, the testimony of a witness was disqualified because of his disbelief in God, the judge declaring, "this belief constituted the sanction of all testimony in a court of justice: and that he knew of no cause in a Christian country, where a witness had been permitted to testify without such belief."[58] Tocqueville noted also that, in the states where the clergy were barred from office, this legislation met the strong approval of the clergy, including Roman Catholic priests. American Roman Catholics were strongly in favor of the American plan, which of course had deep roots in some aspects of medieval thought. The tragic situation for these Roman Catholics arose when intransigent Roman Catholic immigrants attacked both them and Protestants, as well as the American idea, and in part precipitated the wave of anti-Catholicism.

The American sense of destiny, from colonial times to well into the nineteenth century, was a Christian sense of mission and calling. Statist education, after Horace Mann, steadily eroded this faith. The sense of destiny remained in secular form and triumphed in Theodore Roosevelt's

---

[55.] Anson Phelps Stokes, *Church and State in the United States*, vol. I (New York: Harper, 1950), 498.
[56.] Richardson, 222f. In 1802, Hamilton suggested the formation of a Christian Constitutional society and party "devoted to Christianity and the Constitution" to combat Jacobinism and secularism, Louis M. Hacker, *Alexander Hamilton in the American Tradition* (New York: McGraw-Hill, 1957), 237.
[57.] Tocqueville, *op.cit.*, 332.
[58.] *Ibid.*, 334, from the New York Spectator, 23 August 1831.

imperialism. Today, the ideals of the French Revolution govern the federal union, and a world-wide messianic mission of anti-Christian character is the order of the day. But the new order in Washington faces a more consistent expression of the same faith in the Communist Internationale and hence cannot succeed against a more consistent faith without a return to its own basic presuppositions. Meanwhile, the State Department, in censoring military speeches, has struck out of one proposed speech a sentence reading, "We are a Christian Nation."[59] The new faith is unwilling to admit the reality of the old. In legal fact, however, the Christian nature of the United States extensively remains. One scholar, by no means a champion of Christian orthodoxy, has recently added his assent to a description of the position of religion in America as "plural establishment." "No one denomination has legal sanction; all do. Tax and military exemptions, legislative chaplains, and judicial oaths suggest that such establishment is in fact the case."[60] This, however, is an attempt to see the American development in traditional terminology and is correct rather than useful. Establishments did exist, but a new pattern was in process, and the young United States saw itself not only as the fulfilment of past history, but also as the truly new order of history.

The United States of America saw itself as "the new world," not only in the continental sense, but in the Christian sense, as an area of new life, new growth, new possibilities. The literature of immigrants, long after the Christian commonwealth began to fade, retained this sense of newness, this feeling that the ways of Europe were obsolete in a new world. Michael Pupin, in *From Immigrant to Inventor,* recalled "the words of my fellow passenger on the immigrant ship who had said, 'No matter who you are or what you know or what you have you will be a greenhorn when you land in America.'" This sense of American newness is not entirely lost, but it is yielding to an image of the United States as another European imperial power, meddling in international affairs for its own power politics. And, as is so often the case, foreign interventionism has gone hand in hand with domestic intervention and a decline of liberty.

Even legally, however, the old structure still remains to a great extent. Federalism and constitutionalism have enabled the United States to remain the most stable government of the past nearly two centuries.[61] Even Stokes is ready, with qualifications, to recognize that the United States is still in some sense "a Christian nation."[62]

[59.] Bryton Barron, *The Untouchable State Department* (Springfield, Va.: Crestwood Books, 1962), 47.

[60.] Edward Scott Gaustad, *Historical Atlas of Religion in America* (New York: Harper and Row, 1962), 54.

[61.] James Burnham, *Congress and the American Tradition* (Chicago: Regnery, 1959), 66ff.

[62.] Stokes, vol. III, 578.

The Christian Commonwealth concept left its mark on the United States in a deep and continuing fashion. This faith asserted, among other things, five doctrines: first, it affirmed that all law rests on God's fundamental law, so that true laws must be oriented to this higher law. Second, it restricted legal sovereignty to God, and, on the governmental and political levels, made power so diffuse that even a discussion of political sovereignty is made tortuous or irrelevant. Third, as a corollary to the second, it adhered to a limitation of powers in terms of a diverse and federal structure, a concept based both on a distrust of man and a recognition of various areas and spheres of law. Fourth, it held to the doctrine that the civil government can best be Christian by a separation from ecclesiastical government, a faith strongly demanded of the Hebrew Commonwealth of the Old Testament. Fifth, it affirmed the restrictive rather than compulsive role of Christianity, and Sabbath and other such laws were the pride of the young republic. In all these aspects, erosion is extensive, but in every area health is also greater than is generally recognized. The population as a whole regards the United States still as a Christian country. Whereas in Europe as high as one-third of those on church roles are either anti-clerical or vote Communist, in the United States polls show that ninety-six percent consider themselves church members. "In America the unidentified are pro-religious."[63] The greatest sign of health, however, is the rapid rise and growth of Christian schools, an assertion of both Christian faith and of localism. This is an important restoration of local self-government. In many areas, the basic power is within reach: county government. Twelve large population centers today hold one fourth of the population of the United States, and a continuous metropolitan area of almost thirty-eight million people extends from New Hampshire to Virginia.[64] One half of the population is in 220 counties, with the other half in 2800 counties. These 2800 counties in particular represent fairly well developed local cultures. They are dominated by a particular church group, a racial or national background, and an often developed tradition. They are federal units. Their religious and political recovery is in some areas in sight and offers a major hope in terms of a free and Christian society. In England, local authorities are the creatures of Parliament; centralization is now complete. In the United States, this is not true to any degree. Indeed, as seen from the English perspective, localism is still extreme in the United States, not only

63. Franklin Hamlin Littell, *From State Church to Pluralism* (Garden City, N.Y.: Anchor Books, 1962), 161. Littell's position, however, is in contradiction to our thesis. For like data, see Gaustad, *Historical Atlas*, 164.
64. See Jean Gottmann, *Megalopolis, The Urbanized Northeastern Seaboard of the United States* (New York: Twentieth Century Fund, 1961). The city superseded the wilderness as the American frontier. Its growth of late is much slower in the East. Weyl, *The Negro in American Civilization*, 303ff., speaks of the decline of the city, and a flight from it to the suburbs and elsewhere, a flight beginning to affect university life. The city, representing a great capital investment by taxpayers, is increasingly less able to maintain or renew itself as it is invaded by people who find its combination of politics, relief, and subsidies an attraction. In terms of Gresham's law, the good is driven out by the bad, and the city decays.

in civil government but in political parties, so that "no one has ever been able to make himself 'boss' of more than one State, or build an organization extending across a section, nor could a strong President like F. D. Roosevelt act as a 'national party boss.'"[65]

More important, while in the field of religion ecumenicity and church union have been stressed, the stubborn integrity of particular, creedal, and local faith and authority has developed. In spite of bitter attacks and pressures, new church movements are arising in independence of the drive to centralism, and, in most, the emphasis is not only highly creedal and particular, but the church polity is also hostile to centralization. More and more, the missionary movement is in the hands of independent boards. Bible schools and colleges, rapidly increasing in numbers (170 in 1960), and growing in academic stature, are indicative of educational protest, independence, and localism.[66] The growth of the Christian school movement is a major if neglected aspect of present day developments. In the area of newspapers and magazines, as major newspapers and magazines grow fewer, small and dedicated newspapers, newsletters, and magazines increase phenomenally, representing particular perspectives often systematically developed. The restoration of localism and community within the framework of major cities has been ably presented.[67] Thus, although the onslaught against federalism is very great, the resistance to that attack is increasingly virile and intelligent in area after area of thought and activity. Federalism, the unwritten constitution of the United States, is showing extensive signs of regaining both its faith and its vitality.

Long ago, Jedidiah Morse saw the "safety" and "strength" of the United States in its federal nature, which made it a complex variety of structures which could not be reduced to any single description:

> Let us not estimate too lightly *the theory of our government, the constitution of the United States, which has connected itself with the constitutions of the states, and made them constituent parts thereof, thus forming one system,* which, for its originality, its sublimity, and the wonderful combination and adjustments of its principles, possessing all the advantages of a democracy, a republic, and of a confederacy, without any of their prominent evils, cannot fail of exciting the admiration of all succeeding ages.[68]

[65.] M. J. C. Vile, *The Structure of American Federalism* (New York: Oxford University Press, 1961), 94.

[66.] S. A. Witmer, *The Bible College Story: Education with Dimension* (Manhasset, N. Y.: Channel Press, 1962).

[67.] See Jane Jacobs, *The Death and Life of Great American Cities* (New York: Random House, 1961).

[68.] Jedidiah Morse, *Annals of the American Revolution; or a Record of the Causes and Events which Produced and Terminated in the Establishment and Independence of the American Republic* (Hartford, Ct.: 1824), 400. Italics are in original.

9

Democracy and Anarchy

Cynicism and moral relativism are common attitudes in our time. Vinson, as chief justice of the U. S. Supreme Court, asserted, "Nothing is more certain in modern society than the principle that there are no absolutes." The economist Keynes observed, "In the long run, we are all dead." The temper is again, "*Après nous le déluge*," a contempt for the future, so that it is, as Röpke observes, "a virtue to contract debts and ... foolishness to save."[1]

Moreover, pornography, which, in the late eighteenth century began its extensive influence in modern history, has flourished on a widespread scale in recent years, no longer as a vice of the aristocracy, or as an aspect of political or literary illuminism, but on a democratic basis, and as an organized philosophy. Public officials, in prosecuting such works, have seen in the main the sexual content and bluntness and attacked this without a realization of the philosophical import. But, to cite but one example, Henry Miller was never more serious than when he asserted that his concern "was not with sex, nor with religion, but with the problem of self-liberation."[2]

The liberation is from history, Christianity, civilization, and law. A radical moral relativism goes hand in hand with every form of statism and is its instrument and concomitant. This liberation is called a battle for

---

[1] Wilhelm Röpke, *A Humane Economy* (Chicago: Regnery, 1960), 100.
[2] Lawrence Durrell, ed., *The Henry Miller Reader* (New York: New Directions, 1959), 356. On the attitude of the U. S. Supreme Court towards this "self-liberation," see Anthony Lewis, "Sex and the Supreme Court," *Esquire*, vol. LIX, no. 6, June, 1962, 82ff.

liberty, but this "new" definition of liberty is not liberty under law, but rather liberty from law, and it is *anti-law*. Every instance in history of the rise of statism has gone hand in hand with the rise of pornography. The two are closely related. To encourage the one is to further the other. Statism ultimately denies an area of transcendence and insists that man is a social animal and a creature of the state. Law is what the state says it is, so that law in its historic sense, as the revealed will of God, or the principle of order in nature, or as the natural and healthy environment of men and nations, is denied in favor of the naked and arbitrary will of the state. A notable and early example of this link between pornography and statism was the Marquis de Sade, who is widely revered by the modern champions of radical democracy.

In its simpler form, this faith is expressed as "the will of the people." Democracy is "vox populi, vox dei." There is no standard other than the will of the people, which can include all things. It is "the people, yes." Thus Oliver Wendell Holmes saw this concept of democracy as his predominant principle. Speaking to John W. Davis, Solicitor General of the U. S. from 1913 to 1918, Holmes once observed, with reference to the Sherman Act, "Of course I know, and every other sensible man knows, that the Sherman law is damned nonsense, but if my country wants to go to hell, I am here to help it."[3] For Holmes, "truth was the majority vote of that nation that could lick all others."[4] According to Brandeis, Holmes' faith was "that man should be free in a large way. He was a great liberator. He was a great emancipator."[5] True legislation in this sense is giving the people what they want, helping them to get to hell, if they so choose. And greatness or near-greatness, according to Eric F. Goldman, Princeton professor of history, is submission to the popular will, to "the inevitable flow of feeling." Lecturing at Stanford, on August 8, 1962,

> Truman and Eisenhower, Goldman said, will be remembered as "near great" presidents, not because of anything they particularly did, but because they finally, both after "conservative" starts, had "sense enough to not stand in the way of the inevitable flow of feeling in the country."[6]

However, the people, it is held, do not always know what is best for them; true democracy is sometimes not to be confused with ballot box democracy, which may reflect non-democratic ideas.[7] Man's true freedom,

[3] Francis Biddle, *Justice Holmes, Natural Law, and the Supreme Court* (New York: Macmillan, 1961), 8f.
[4] *Ibid.*, 46f.
[5] *Ibid.*, 18.
[6] Dan Schwartz, "WWII Changes Feelings About Policies: Goldman," *Stanford Summer Weekly*, vol. 8, no. 7, 9 August 1962, 1.
[7] See R. J. Rushdoony, *The Messianic Character of American Education* (Nutley, N.J.: The Craig Press, 1963) for educational theories holding this position.

moreover, involves state control over vast areas of private activity. As Walter Reuther has said, "Only a moron would believe that the millions of private economic decisions being made independently of each other will somehow harmonize in the end and bring us out where we want to be." Government intervention and control is necessary.[8] Thus statism is born out of man's retreat from responsibility, and *every retreat from responsibility is a denial of accountability and its concomitant, law.* God alone is truly beyond responsibility, having no law beyond Himself, being Himself law, holiness, righteousness, and truth. For man to seek life beyond law, beyond good and evil, is to claim to be a god, and, at the same time, to abdicate manhood, which means capability and responsibility under God. The caretaker state is the refuge and liberation of these champions of anti-law. The caretaker state seeks to transcend or abolish history; it seeks to create the final and perfect order and usher man into paradise regained, and regained without God. But, to run from history is to run from responsibility, and to evade responsibility is to evade manhood.

The religious and philosophical roots of this position are very extensive. John Dewey emphatically affirmed this war against law. Supernatural Christianity and democracy are inevitably enemies, as Dewey recognized. Any concept of an absolute law or justice, any standard in terms of which men were judged and separated as Godly or wicked, as "the saved and the lost," meant a "spiritual aristocracy." "I cannot understand how any realization of the democratic ideal as a vital moral and spiritual ideal in human affairs is possible without surrender of the conception of the basic division to which supernatural Christianity is committed."[9] Values are thus anti-democratic, as is school grading. Prisons condemn evil actions, which are seen as nonexistent; either mental rehabilitation must replace prisons, or, with anarchists, total democracy and no condemnation whatsoever. War and nationalism are, like values, divisive; they too must be eliminated, since nothing is worth fighting for, and every boundary and definition is inherently false. And, in Miller's words, "Morality is for slaves, beings without spirit....Evil does not exist."[10]

This too is the faith of theological neo-orthodoxy and existentialism. Thus, Karl Barth's doctrine of the "freedom" of God is God's ostensible freedom from law, from any eternal counsel, from the necessity to regard as holy tomorrow that which is deemed so today. Again, Barth's doctrine

---

[8.] Lawrence Fertig, "Free Economy 'Only for Morons?,'" *N. Y. World Telegram and Sun*, 20 August 1962.

[9.] John Dewey, *A Common Faith* (New Haven, Ct.: Yale University Press, 1934), 84.

[10.] Henry Miller, *Tropic of Cancer* (New York: Grove Press, 1961), xvi. Note, in this respect, William Saroyan's statement: "In 1935, in the great wastes of America, undiscovered, there shall be inward laughter and endless innocence, and it is so, Lord, and none is with guilt. In this joyous hour of deepest grief, not even the most evil are with guilt, Lord," *A Christmas Psalm, 1935.*

of "election" has strong implications of total democracy. The dynamic of his theology is the dynamic of relativism and change. As the United Presbyterian Church has stated it, "It must be recognized anew that our God is a dynamic Lord, a truly unpredictable source of ongoing revelation."[11] This "ongoing revelation," being "truly unpredictable," can call "truth" tomorrow that which is a "lie" for today; all values are thus relative, and being alone has reality. The total movement is thus anti-law, anti-value, and anti-meaning, for the insistence on meaning is a demand for rationality, logic, and predictability, things which by nature are said to be alien to God and hence alien to reality. It is a source of triumph in the modern arts, therefore, to war against meaning. Thus, a poem should not *mean*, it is. To cherish law, value, and meaning is to be a Philistine and a vulgarian according to this inverse snobbery which wages a war against everything which divides men in terms of an absolute standard. There is thus a democracy of meaning, a levelling of man and of institutions, and a subordination of all things to the idea of democracy and its organized form, the state. In terms of this faith, Conant can view the family as an institution which frustrates egalitarianism:

> Wherever the institution of the family is still a powerful force, as it is in this country, surely *inequality* of opportunity is automatically, and often unconsciously, a basic principal of the nation; the more favored parents endeavor to obtain even greater favors for their children. Therefore, when we Americans proclaim an adherence to the doctrine of equality of opportunity, we face the necessity for a perpetual compromise. Now it seems to me important to recognize both the inevitable conflict and the continuing nature of the compromise.[12]

Conant perhaps sees a continuing compromise as needful in view of our cultural context. Others see no such need for compromise, and, more consistently, see the family as necessarily doomed if true democracy is to prevail.

Another major source for this concept of total democracy is Albert Schweitzer, whose philosophy is by his own affirmation derived from the Enlightenment rather than Christianity. The philosophy of "reverence for life" eliminates ethics by equalizing all being into a total democracy of life. It is Schweitzer's hope, having equalized being, that men will be loving, that they will respect and revere life in its every form, but he fails to see any law other than the total democracy of life. What Schweitzer has affirmed

---

11. From an unapproved, but not so stated, Report to the 174th General Assembly of the United Presbyterian Church, passed on nonetheless for study "by synods, presbyteries, and sessions." "Relations Between Church and State," *Presbyterian Life*, 15 (1 September 1962), 28.
12. James Bryant Conant, *Education in a Divided World, The Function of the Public Schools in our Unique Society* (Cambridge, Mass.: Harvard University Press, 1948), 8. See, by way of contrast, Anthony M. Ludovici, *The False Assumptions of "Democracy"* (London: Heath Cranton, 1921).

in his philosophy, Henry Miller has more consistently applied. He is, in his own words, religious "without espousing any religion.... That means simply having a reverence for life, being on the side of life instead of death. Again, the word 'civilization' to my mind is coupled with death. When I use the word, I see civilization as a crippling, thwarting thing, a stultifying thing."[13] Miller is one of a number of writers and artists who have applied the idea of total democracy with radical thoroughness. Others have talked of it while they have insistently lived it. Paris, with its continuing revolutionary ideology, is their homeland. Their literary forebears include men like Rimbaud, who sought by systematic debauchery and homosexuality to place himself beyond good and evil, to break down the control of reason and normal inhibitions, to be, in short, the "damned" of God so that he might by his illuminism remake himself and humanity into the true god: "I am he who will create God!"[14]

Walt Whitman, who was not without his French inspiration,[15] as well as verbal affectations (Salut au Monde, Respondez, allons, etc.), affirmed the same faith and expressed his own perversion in verse. His denial of values and affirmation of total democracy is continuously in view, best known perhaps in "To a Common Prostitute," "Not till the sun excludes you, do I exclude you." Nature is normative; all that has being *is* being and equally "good," if such language can be used. Thus, in his poem "Walt Whitman," he expresses contempt for civilization, religion, property, and work, while delighting in animals because "they are so placid and self-contain'd." In "Respondez!" he declares, "Let faces and theories be turn'd inside out! let meanings be freely criminal, as well as results!...Let the earth desert God, nor let there ever henceforth be mention'd the name of God! Let there be no God!" For Miller, Whitman was "the first and the last poet."[16]

What Whitman called for, Miller became. He affirms a war on civilization, reason, and logic. He hates cleanliness and righteousness. Miller's summons is to "abdicate...scrap the past instantly." As against Jehovah, the Great I AM, Miller declares "I am," and his book is "not a book" but "a prolonged insult, a gob of spit in the face of Art, a kick in the pants to God, Man, Destiny, Time, Love, Beauty... what you will." To all that law and civilization represent, he is a "hyena," a scavenger waiting to destroy and devour its carcass. Hence his delight in affirming, "I am proud to say that I am inhuman."[17] Hence too his delight in relating his sexuality, theft, and contempt for decency. "I've liked only what is alien....obscenity

---

13. George Wickes, "Henry Miller at Seventy," an interview, *Claremont Quarterly,* 9 (Winter 1962), 13.
14. Enid Starkie, *Arthur Rimbaud* (New York: New Directions, 1961), 85f., 100ff., 108, 122, 176, 183ff.
15. See Esther Shephard, *Walt Whitman's Pose* (New York: Harcourt Brace, 1938).
16. Miller, *Tropic of Cancer*, 240.
17. *Ibid.*, xxv, 1f, 98f., 254ff.

is a cleansing process, whereas pornography only adds to the murk....
Whenever a taboo is broken, something good happens, something
vitalizing."[18] This is a demand for the primitive saturnalia, the
revitalization of society by the ritual return to chaos. This too is the
rationale of revolution: regeneration is to be achieved through the cleansing
bloodbath of chaos. The return to paradise is through the destruction of
history, meaning, and morality. The "time of the assassins" must come
again, a ruthless destruction of all things, so that a new world, characterized
by anarchy, racial amalgamation, and universal human hermaphroditism
("the birth of male-and-female in every individual"), may dawn.[19] Anarchy
and decay are thus approved.[20] Not surprisingly, Miller speaks of meeting
Emma Goldman, the anarchist, in 1913, as his "turning point in life."[21]
Again, it is not surprising that the radical relativism of Far Eastern cultural
collapse, Zen Buddhism, is influential among the thinkers of radical
democracy. It is again not surprising that Miller, who once planned to write
"a new Bible—*The Last Book*,"[22] should declare also, "I would welcome the
day when the film would displace literature, when there'd be no more need
to read."[23] This then is a religious faith, and Miller describes his acceptance
of it as a rebirth preceded by a kind of crucifixion.[24] Peace comes through
a surrender of all standards, morality, religion, and selfhood.[25] "I believe in
absolute freedom of expression."[26] "The test of a man's humanity lies in his
acceptance of life, all aspects of life, not just those which correspond with
his own limited viewpoint. As dear old sadly misunderstood Nietzsche
said—The Yea-sayers!"[27] This means saying "yea" to every appetite and is a
means of attaining salvation. This new religion alone will "save" man;
hence, an anthology of Miller's philosophy was compiled, a reader, as a
new "bible," with the suggestion of putting "one in every hotel room in
America, after removing the Gideon Bibles and placing them in the laundry
chutes."[28] Miller is the new and true "holy man."[29] White dreamed of a
school using such a reader for "the liberating and purifying effects these
books have had upon young and old alike." For him, Miller is a "superman

---

[18.] Wickes, 12.
[19.] Durrell, *The Henry Miller Reader*, 231-239.
[20.] *Ibid.*, 250, 256, 263.
[21.] *Ibid.*, 384. See Richard Drinnon, *Rebel in Paradise, A Biography of Emma Gold-man* (Chicago: University of Chicago Press, 1961), 164.
[22.] Miller, *Tropic of Cancer*, 26.
[23.] Wickes, 17.
[24.] *Ibid.*, 19.
[25.] Durell, 56, 61.
[26.] Henry Miller, "First Reply to Trygve Hirsch," in Emil White, ed., *Henry Miller Between Heaven and Hell* (Big Sur, Calif.: Emil White, 1961), 11.
[27.] *Ibid.*, 16. When Miller speaks of a "conscience," and "of an Absolute, of law," he has reference to this urge to say "yea" to life; see Miller, *The Wisdom of the Heart* (Norfolk, Conn.: New Directions, 1960), 88.
[28.] Karl Shapiro, "The Greatest Living Author," in *The Henry Miller Reader*, v.
[29.] *Ibid.*, xv.

and prophet."[30] For Peter P. Rohde, Miller's mysticism will reestablish the link between human and divine, and Miller is to be compared to Buddha, Jesus, and St. Francis.[31] Albert Maillet goes further: "his readers sometimes see in him a Christ, a God. And indeed, there is a great deal of truth in this opinion." He is "the appearance of a new type of man.... We are reminded of the coming of Christ." Christ's prophecy is "realized in the works of de Sade and Miller," which fulfill what the French and Russian revolutions failed to do. Maillet seems to apologize for the absence of a perversion in Miller, Whitman's homosexuality, but this is "a simple question of temperament." "In the end divinity will be fully realized, not only in one man such as Miller, but in all mankind. I find the same kind of salvation prophesied in the Gospel."[32]

The number of men who have made pilgrimages to Miller in Paris, Big Sur, and Beverly Glen form an impressive list of notables of our time, writers, artists, thinkers, and even political figures. University scholars have refused to testify against Miller, and many, such as Mark Schorer and Eugene Burdick, have testified in his favor, as did the United Presbyterian professor of systematic theology at the San Francisco Theological Seminary, San Anselmo, California, Arnold Come. Come found that Miller "has, by his daring...contributed to a new freedom in American literature toward the very serious problems of sex and social conformity."[33]

What was this new freedom? Walt Whitman in his old age described his "poetic method" as the "notion of receptivity to experience, and of a complete surrender to it, combined with a patient effort to grasp its deepest meaning."[34] The background to this was not only the Enlightenment exaltation of man, but Romanticism's enthronement of experience. Darwin, Freud, and Jung furthered the development by reading the significant area of experience back into the biological ancestry, the racial

[30.] White, 4f.

[31.] Rohde, in White, 50-58.

[32.] Maillet, "Henry Miller, Superman and Prophet," *ibid.*, 59-85.

[33.] Donovan Bess, "Miller's 'Tropic' on Trial," *Evergreen Review*, 6, no. 23 (March-April, 1962), 24. Bess, in the course of his article on the Marin County trial, quotes as oracle *The San Francisco Chronicle*, not adding that he wrote for the *Chronicle*. The ecclesiastical defenses of prosecuted books are an interesting aspect of recent history. In the May 1, 1962, number of *Presbyterian Life*, Robert McAfee Brown held *Lady Chatterley's Lover*, among other works, to be a source of truth from God. In England, in 1961, the Bishop of Woolwich called *Lady Chatterley's Lover* "a book all Christians should read" and became known thereby as the Chatterley bishop. Either through "innocence" or failure to read the book, both churchmen failed to realize that the central freedom desired and attained in Lawrence's tract-novel is not adultery, which is taken for granted, but anal intercourse. Concerning the meaning of Lawrence's novel, see Ralph Ginzburg, "The Secret Message of Lady Chatterley's Lover," *Eros*, 1 (Summer 1962), 25-27.

[34.] As summarized and reported by Logan Pearsall Smith, *Unforgotten Years* (Boston: Little, Brown, 1939), 105.

unconscious, and the individual unconscious. The new locus of infallibility, once resting in God and His Scripture, was now the unconscious, whose infallible word, in Freudian slips, asserted itself against the sickly and error-ridden consciousness of man. Many were quick to see, in spite of the illogical restraints imposed by their mentors, that the new freedom was, in Whitman's fashion, a complete receptivity and surrender to experience without any interposition of "sickly" restraints such as Christianity and its morality. The holy men of this faith, its desert fathers, became the "Beats," the blessed ones, whose "whole idea was to experience *holiness*...the beatific vision...orgiastic release...the crucifixion of the flesh."[35] In terms of this faith, moral judgments with reference to perversions, Christian standards with reference to ultimate law, God's sovereignty and judgment, social judgments concerning narcotics, and political hopes for justice, are all aspects of the Social Lie and hindrances to either the physical or the "metaphysical orgasm." Whores are "the *original* hipsters—the outlaws, the outcasts." In terms of "The Gospel According to Anthropology and Prehistory," the old gods of civilization are all obsolete. The new god is in man's unconscious, not in his civilized accretions, and, in terms of this, the writing of one "Beat" on a mirror is to be understood: "This is the face of God you see."[36] Not immorality but amorality is cultivated as "the way."

Another champion of the same faith is Allen Ginsberg, author of *Howl, For Carl Solomon*, who has sought experience in drugs[37] and in sexual experimentation, and has expressed his contempt of civilized ways by public nakedness.[38] At the trial of Ginsberg's *Howl*, academic notables were again arrayed on the side of the defense, Mark Schorer and others appearing to defend the author. Kenneth Rexroth, poet and *San Francisco Examiner* columnist, described *Howl* as "prophetic" writing, comparable to that of the Biblical prophets. The theme of *Howl*, according to Rexroth, is simply that "Everything that is human is Holy to me," and that salvation rests in "the love of everything Holy in man." Herbert Blau, of the San Francisco State College faculty, described *Howl* as "a vision that by the salvation of despair, by the salvation of what would appear to be perversity, by the salvation of what would appear to be obscene, by the salvation of what would appear to be illicit, is ultimately a kind of redemption of the illicit, the obscene, the disillusioned and the despairing."[39] Salvation is thus

---

[35.] Lawrence Lipton, *The Holy Barbarians* (New York: Messner, 1959), 81.

[36.] *Ibid.*, 48, 123, 162ff.

[37.] See Allen Ginsberg, in David Ebin, ed., *The Drug Experience* (New York: Orion, 1961), 301-307.

[38.] Described by Lipton, 193-205, as "The New Apocalypse."

[39.] From excerpts of testimony reported in *Evergreen Review*, 1 no. 4 (New York: Grove Press), 154f., 195f. In Ginsberg's "Footnote to Howl," this is clearly stated: "Everything is holy, everybody's holy, everywhere is holy!," in Thomas Parkinson, ed., *A Casebook on the Beat* (New York: Crowell, 1961), 12; cf. 172, Michael McClure: "There are no categories! or justifications!"

the total acceptance of all that Biblical faith condemns, and the total rejection of Biblical Christianity. Redemption is deliverance from God's sovereign law to man's law, to the totalitarian authority of the underground, the subconscious, the subversive, the outlaw, and the criminal.

Relativism was manifest in the editing of the *Webster's Third New International Dictionary* in 1961. All usage was given almost equal status, so that standard English is in effect slighted. Ironically, one of the critics of this dictionary, which implicitly outlawed any preceptive teaching of English, was Mark Schorer, defender of the same principle in Miller and Ginsberg!

This new faith was not without its immediate popularization in a variety of ways, as witness Rey Anthony's *The Housewife's Handbook on Selective Promiscuity.* Mrs. Anthony, "on the basis of her own extensive and intensive sex experiences," offers a handbook on the subject to others, and, among other things, writes "unprudishly to indicate the advantages of anal stimulation and sexual varietism."

This temper is championed in literature and life. Thus, William Carlos Williams, in his introduction to *The Lover and other poems* by Mimi Goldberg (1961), declares, "A woman has to give herself without question when the mood is upon her. She cannot question herself, what she is transcribing." As a result of this temper, we have what Nicanor Parra of Chile calls *Anti-Poems.*[40] Academic poets, at times able to write lovely lyrics, turn increasingly to anti-poetry for their medium, as witness Theodore Roethke. Among students, this philosophical anarchism and relativism is widespread.[41]

This anarchism is of course closely related to statism. The denial of God's sovereignty and the affirmation of man's sovereignty (whether of rational or irrational man or of his unconscious being) denies transcendence and leaves only two realities, individual man and collective man. In the name of individual man, collective man, the state, establishes its total order and absolute tyranny.

[40.] English translation by Jorge Elliott, (San Francisco, Calif.: City Lights Books, 1960).

[41.] See David Horowitz, *Student* (New York: Ballantine, 1962). Horowitz champions this movement. In a *Daily Pennsylvanian* article, Steve Foster condemned the HUAC and suggested that we be free "to advocate *anything* including Communism, cannibalism, and ritual incest"; see *Analysis*, 1, no. 1, (April 1961), 6; University of Pennsylvania, Eleutherian Society publication. There were elements of the same philosophical anarchism in various student defenses of Dr. Leo Koch, a University of California alumnus, when he was dismissed as assistant professor of biology at the University of Illinois; see Horowitz, 21, 36f. For the link between anarchism and collectivism, see Miller's mystical concept of this in *The Wisdom of the Heart*, 78-93.

This new faith is not limited to literature but is also operative in the sciences, where Kinsey provides the most obvious instance. Kinsey, operating in terms of a democracy of values, was able to classify homosexuality and "animal contacts" with normal marital sexual relations as equally valid since equally natural. Since nature is normative, no law beyond nature is admissible, and we have a new meaning given to Deism's old faith that whatever is, is right.

Total democracy means total "equality" and the end of morality and values as divisive and aristocratic. The goal is total levelling. In the transitional stage, for Marxism in its various forms, a dictatorship of the proletariat is necessary to eradicate God and history, and it is permitted as a means to the end. In the liberal tradition, the same hope for a dictatorship was expressed by Col. Edward Mandell House (1858-1938) in his political novel, *Philip Dru: Administrator* (1912). In various forms, the hope expresses itself. Science, education, wonder drugs, and other human devices will invalidate differences and usher in total democracy. In education, grades are seen as divisive and anti-democratic in terms of this faith. In welfare, subsidy is the order of the day to equalize all; the excellence of the superior is an offense for which they must be taxed to reward the failure of others. Values are anti-democratic. But this new democracy has steadily created the most extreme aristocracy in history and the greatest cultural gap. As Diana Spearman has observed, "The century of the common man is distinguished by the most aristocratic culture that has ever existed, aristocratic in the sense that it has no popular roots and that the average person can neither understand nor enjoy it."[42] Whether in painting, literature, music, or other areas, popular taste is despised by the artist and an esoteric art created demanding interpretation by experts only. "All this may seem remote from politics, but submission to the demands of experts for only half-comprehended reasons makes people willing to accept the orders, legislation or policy of any popularly elected Government."[43] Experts are elected and then meekly submitted to. The experts thus become a dictatorship of the proletariat, ostensibly guiding them for their own welfare. This new aristocracy, whose inverse snobbery is its contempt of all Christian values in the name of anti-values, deliberately cuts itself off from the masses who are still wedded to *meaning* and to *value*. To cherish these is to be moral, Christian, a vulgarian, and a Philistine, and no greater sin can exist in the eyes of this new Islam. Total war must be waged against God, against all meaning, value, morality, law, and order, in short, against everything that divides men in terms of an absolute standard. It is productive of political chaos by its attack on the idea of law. This planned

---

[42.] Diana Spearman, *Democracy in England* (New York: Macmillan, 1957), 160.
[43.] *Ibid.*, 162.

chaos characterized the first step of both the Russian and French revolutions and is the prelude to the new law of the total state.

The role of Freud, who compared himself to Copernicus and Galileo, has been mentioned. Freud held belief in "psychic freedom and choice" to be "quite unscientific," and his followers have been characterized by "their relative freedom from concern about the ethical implications of their central positions."[44] In terms of this studied irresponsibility, "a vast reorganization of the world" is demanded by many psychiatrists and champions of "mental health."[45]

A more basic influence has been that of Darwin, whose evolutionary hypothesis provided a framework for assault on orthodox Christian faith and a free market economy to the Union League advocates of radical Reconstruction in the South, to John D. Rockefeller, Andrew Carnegie, and the various industrialists who bypassed old-fashioned Christianity, constitutionalism, and capitalism with their neo-Mercantilism.

Evolution is a genetic faith and makes the prior, which is the primitive, determinative; the primitive is more basic, hence more vital and real. It follows therefore that sex is more important then religion, since sex appears early on the evolutionary ladder, and religion is a latecomer. Rationality is thus less significant than emotion, since rationality is a late arrival. Hence Miller regards movies as superior to books and hopes to eliminate books. Some also hold monogamy to be a late "arrival"; hence, true sexuality is possible, the "Beats" assert, in an anti-moral, anti-Christian context, as amorality rather than immorality. Genetic psychology explains reason by emotion and emotion by the subconscious. It explains civilized man by primitive man, man in general by animals, and animals by the evolutionary process. The result is what Cornelius Van Til has aptly termed "integration into the void."[46] As Miller stated it, "You see, I think it's bad to think."[47] Man is dissolved into the void—and into the arms of the caretaker state. The result is a democracy of tyranny. Divisions are intolerable; men cannot be separated from one another; nothing is worth fighting for. The new Tower of Babel is in process.

As against this, the only refuge and strength of man is in the sovereignty of God and His infallible word, in the absolute law of God. We are either believers in this God, or we take a road which leads to radical and total democracy. The weakness of the United States today is its halfway

---

[44.] Elton Trueblood, "Contemporary Psychiatry and the Concept of Responsibility" in Helmut Schoeck and James W. Wiggins, eds., *Psychiatry and Responsibility* (Princeton, N.J.: Van Nostrand, 1962), 21.

[45.] See Hervey M. Cleckley, "Psychiatry: Science, Art, and Scientism" in Schoeck and Wiggins, 83-116.

[46.] See C. Van Til, *The Psychology of Religion* (Philadelphia: Presbyterian and Reformed Publications).

[47.] Wickes, 9.

position, a stand lacking the strength of either faith. The irrelevance and judgment of the lukewarm was long ago indicated by Christ: "So then because thou art lukewarm, and neither cold nor hot, I will spue thee out of my mouth" (Rev. 3:16).

10

The French Revolution
and the American Conservative
Counter-Revolution

Drucker some years ago challenged as "fallacious" the belief that the origins of the American Revolution were to be found in the Enlightenment, and denied also that the American Revolution was a forerunner of the French. Instead, he asserted,

> The American Revolution was based on principles completely contrary to those of the Enlightenment and the French Revolution. In intention and effect it was a successful countermovement against the very rationalist despotism of the Enlightenment which provided the political foundation for the French Revolution. Though the French Revolution happened later in time, it had politically and philosophically been anticipated by the American Revolution. The conservatives of 1776 and 1787 fought and overcame the spirit of the French Revolution so that the American development actually represents a more advanced stage in history than the *Etats Generaux,* the Terror, and Napoleon. Far from being a revolt against the old tyranny of feudalism, the American Revolution was a conservative counterrevolution in the name of freedom against the new tyranny of rationalist liberalism and Enlightened Despotism.

> ... The Freedom of the Western world during the nineteenth century and up to this day has been based upon the ideas, principles, and institutions of the American conservative counterrevolution of 1776.

> The American Revolution brought victory and power to a group which in Europe had been almost completely defeated and which was apparently dying out rapidly: the anticentralist, antitotalitarian

conservatives with their hostility to absolute and centralized government and their distrust of any ruler claiming perfection.[1]

The success of the American Revolution, adds Drucker, defeated the Enlightenment in England and enabled the conservative thought of Burke to gain ascendancy there.[2] Drucker's characterization of the American revolt as the "conservative counterrevolution" is perhaps the best single description of that cause. The attempts of Beard, Jameson, Parrington, and others to read a contrary temper into the American Revolution cannot be sustained. Malin's blunt judgment with reference to Parrington is clearly in order:

> The most conspicuous example of this combined social science-literary degradation of American history was Vernon L. Parrington's *Main Currents of American Thought*. It belongs to the same class as Hitler's *Mein Kampf* in debasing history to the level of vicious propaganda in support of a social program being imposed upon a nation.[3]

The differences between the two revolutions were noted by many persons other than Burke. Thus Friedrich Gentz (1764-1832), adviser to Metternich and secretary to the Congress of Vienna, in 1810 called attention to four essential differences. First, the American Revolution was grounded upon firmly established legal principles and traditions, whereas the French Revolution moved on obviously illegal and unprincipled premises. Second, the American Revolution was *"defensive,"* a battle by Americans to preserve their liberties and continue their legitimate development, whereas the French was "from beginning to end, in the highest sense of the word, an offensive revolution." Third, the American Revolution had a fixed, definite, limited, and particularistic objective, whereas the French had none, but rather moved in terms of "arbitrary will, and of a boundless anarchy." Fourth, the American Revolution, because of

---

[1] Peter F. Drucker, *The Future of Industrial Man* (New York: John Day, 1942), 219, 222f. Marxists also, with a different emphasis, have seen the counterrevolutionary aspect, but view it as a conspiracy of some men against the American Revolution and its soldiers. According to one American, "That the Constitution and the Government of the United States were established not through Revolution but through Counter-Revolution could be seen by the type of government that was set up under Washington and Adams," Albert Weisbord, *The Conquest of Power, Liberalism Anarchism, Syndicalism, Socialism, Fascism and Communism*, vol. I (New York: Covici Friede, 1937), 75. As against this, the whole of American colonial history, culminating in the rebellion and the United States, is clearly a conservative counter-revolution against the direction of English, and European, history. And, as Clinton Rossiter has observed, "The Constitution was a triumph for Conservatism, but not for reaction," *Conservatism in America, The Thankless Persuasion*, second edition revised (New York: Vintage, 1962), 104.

[2] *Ibid.*, 224. Carl Bridenbaugh, in contrast, tries to see the Revolution as a product of the Enlightenment in *Cities in Revolt, Urban Life in America, 1773-1776* (New York: Alfred A. Knopf, 1955), 425.

[3] James C. Malin, *On the Nature of History, Essays about History and Dissidence* (Ann Arbor, Mich.: J.W. Edwards, 1954), 30f.

its limited and legal nature, met with limited resistance, whereas the French could only "force its way by violence and crimes."[4]

The New Englander, Thomas Paine (who changed his name to Robert Treat Paine to avoid confusion with the Englishman who wrote the *Rights of Man),* in "Adams and Liberty" (1798), written when war with France seemed imminent, saw the difference as one between "Anarch's pestilent worm" and America's "laws" and her long tradition, which he compared to "imperial oak; whose roots, like our liberties, ages have nourished."

> While France her huge limbs bathes recumbent in blood,
>   And Society's base threats with wide dissolution;
> May Peace like the dove, who returned from the flood,
>   Find an ark of abode in our mild constitution.
>
> 'Tis the fire of the flint, each American warms.
>   Let Rome's haughty victors beware of collision,
> Let them bring all the vassals of Europe in arms,
>   We're a world by ourselves, and disdain a division.[5]

The French Revolution represented the violent culmination of three major forces. First, the ideas of the Enlightenment found their major expression and application in a radical and thorough fashion in the French Revolution. It was seen as man's opportunity to reorder history and remake man in terms of the light of this philosophy. Second, it was the triumph as well as the blood bath hope of various illuminist societies, secret and subversive, dedicated to the same faith as the Enlightenment philosophers but with organizational strategies added.[6] Third, it represented the culmination also of a statist tradition in France. Extensive social legislation in the face of unemployment, famine, flood, fire, epizootics, and plague, and which established hospitals, asylums, family welfare, educational aid, pensions, and the like, characterized the French monarchy. Private charity and individual responsibility were steadily replaced by welfare legislation. The Revolution thus presented itself as the total caretaker state, in fulfilment of what the monarchy had begun.

[4.] Friedrich Gentz, translated by John Quincy Adams, "The French and American Revolutions Compared," in S. T. Possony, *Three Revolutions* (Chicago: Regnery, 1959).

[5.] Albert Bushnell Hart, *American History Told by Contemporaries,* vol. III (New York: Macmillan, 1897), 319-321. As against this, one of the most conservative of New Englanders was, curiously, favorable to the French Revolution as a blow to despotism; see Edmund S. Morgan, *The Gentle Puritan, A Life of Ezra Stiles, 1727-1795* (New Haven, Ct.: Yale University Press, 1962), 455-461. On September 4, 1823, Jefferson wrote to Adams in favor of world revolution, seeing its results as "worth rivers of blood and years of desolation," *The Adams-Jefferson Letters, The Complete Correspondence Between Thomas Jefferson and Abigail and John Adams,* vol. II, (Chapel Hill: University of North Carolina Press, 1959), 596.

[6.] See Una Birch, *Secret Societies and the French Revolution* (London: John Lane, 1911), 3-63; and Nesta H. Webster, *The French Revolution, A Study in Democracy* (London: Constable, 1921).

From the early days of the Revolution relief was declared to be a national obligation, a debt that the state owed to its citizens. In words the Revolutionists probably went further than the Old Regime, but in deeds they merely followed policy that had long been established under the Old Regime.[7]

In England, however, these problems were steadily met in the sixteenth and seventeenth centuries by an immense outpouring of private, charitable wealth, so that educational, charitable, and reforming goals were achieved through societal rather than statist agencies. The result was "a quiet but veritable revolution."[8] The American tradition represents a continuation of this English "revolution," and the extensive development of associations, charities, foundations, colleges, schools, and the world wide missionary movement are aspects of this progression.

The three major expressions of the philosophy of the Enlightenment have been, first, the French Revolution; second, Darwin and the mythology of evolution; and, third, the Russian Revolution and its Marxian theories. A number of premises and presuppositions govern this developed faith, and an understanding of them is basic to a comprehension of contemporary history.

First, this philosophy implies a rejection of the past and of history. "The French Revolution, which felt the need of a new Year One and a new calendar, was a revolution against history."[9] According to this faith, God's time must be supplanted by man's time, and God's total government and decree by man's total government and decree. This philosophy holds that the clean slate concept of mind is basic to true education, so that education is not development but conditioning. This concept, applied to history, sees revolution as the historical clean slate: the past is wiped out, in order that history may begin afresh. With the French, a new calendar marked a new era in time. The culmination of this new time, the revolutionary era, will be, for Marxism and the Communist International, the end of history. Whether justified in the name of reason (before Darwin) or of science (after Darwin), the philosophy of the Enlightenment is antihistorical. Burke opposed the French Revolution because of its antihistorical and anti-Christian nature, but supported the American Revolution because it was the true fulfilment of a Christian development and history. The clean

[7.] Shelby T. McCloy, *Government Assistance in Eighteenth-Century France* (Durham, N.C.: Duke University Press, 1946), 276.
[8.] W. K. Jordan, *Philanthropy in England, 1480-1660, A Study of the Changing Pattern of English Social Aspirations* (London: George, Allen and Unwin, 1959), 240.
[9.] Pieter Geyl, *Use and Abuse of History* (New Haven, Ct.: Yale University Press, 1955), 22. The consequence is a studied rootlessness fostered by education. Because of this rootlessness, "The educated strata are more gullible than the less educated. The most enthusiastic supporters of Marxism, Nazism, and Fascism were the intellectuals, not the boors," Ludwig von Mises, *Bureaucracy* (New Haven, Ct: Yale University Press, 1946), 108.

slate conception of the mind had ancient roots, but it came into its own in the Enlightenment.

Second, as a corollary to the first, there is a rejection of institutions and customs inherited from the past which are deemed to be either non-rational or unscientific. As a result, there is a hostility to religion, marriage, and the family in terms of this faith, a hostility to everything, indeed, except the state. Everything is thus eroded down to two components, man and the state, and man is the creature of the state and has no transcendence in relation to it.

Third, evil is not in human nature, which is either good or at least neutral, but is in the environment. Man is hence malleable. The state, by reordering the environment, will be able to create a perfect humanity. "By changing human institutions human nature itself will be born again."[10] Redemption is thus political action, not religious faith, and statism is made necessary to man. Horace Mann held that state schools would eliminate crime, slums, prisons, and all human ills; socialists hold that state actions will accomplish the same purpose through politico-economic legislation; the champions of a welfare economy or interventionism believe that housing projects will end slums, poverty, and delinquency. With every form of this faith, empiricism prevails: external measures and impressions will govern the mind and nature of man, which is essentially passive. Even the creative rationalism of Kant is at this point empirical: it rests on the prior empirical experience which then leads to a creative response. As against all this, the U. S. Constitution was not written in terms of any faith in the essential goodness of man, an article of the new faith, but in terms of checks and balances, a distrust in man.

Fourth, the new managers of society must be scientists, educators, and politicians, the new philosopher kings, men who move in terms of science and "scientific" education, political theory, and economics. These, whether called planners, managers, civil servants, or the dictatorship of the proletariat, are assumed to be able to institute efficacious control and alter the nature of man by proper state action. This elite, moving in terms of reason or science, can remake man and society. It is seen, not as a power elite, but as objective and selfless, and as expression of scientific reason.

Fifth, it is held by this philosophy that man and society are basically secular, non-theistic or atheistic, rather than religious. Therefore Christianity is at best peripheral rather than essential to man, society, and

---

10. Louis I. Bredvold, *The Brave New World of the Enlightenment* (Ann Arbor, Mich.: The University of Michigan Press, 1961), 112. For a Czech theological perspective on this expectation, see Jan Michalko on "The Church in a Socialist Society," *Dialog*, 2, no. 3 (Summer 1963), 224-231. Michalko believes that the church must not only coexist but also cooperate with socialism while maintaining a "dialogue."

civil government. Modern society is thus non-religious or irreligious by principle.

Sixth, the supremacy of science is asserted. Comte saw three stages of thought: first, the theological or fictitious; second, the metaphysical or abstract; third, scientific or positive thought. Comte's formulation sharpened a long-developing faith. More important, Comte, in holding that scientific thought is not concerned with causes, or meaning, as the means to desired results, thereby furthered *the triumph of methodology over meaning*. Hence, methodology is more important than content in scientific education. Hence also the extensive unconcern of scientists with the meaning of their activity; science is methodology. Hence, again, the establishment of democracy is seen as the cure-all for all cultures, since methodology will remake man. Democracy is thus applied to Asiatic, African, and Latin American states without any regard for their historical and cultural conditions, because it is assumed that the form or method is the creator of valid objectives. This concept governs the United Nations and U. S. State Department policies, and the activities of the Communist International as well. Methodology is creative and has priority. Methodology then imposes a radically different conception of life upon man. Methodology is both functional and economical. It is concerned with the shortest distance between two points. It wants to eliminate what seems to be unessential from this scientific perspective. The family and private property are both uneconomical and non-functional in this sense and must be eliminated. Test-tube babies, or controlled heredity, have thus been proposed as more efficient. Indeed, it has even been suggested that men be wired at birth, with sockets, for central agency control. Total planning and control are inescapable conclusions of this priority of methodology. So, too, is simplism. Bark has called attention to one of the central failures of Rome, the confusion of "simplicity with strength, as if one could not exist without the other."[11] This Roman hunger for simplicity has been surpassed in the scientific ideal of simplicity *in hypothesis and method*, a religious axiom in essence. This triumph of methodology has been erosive of everything except the power of the scientific state to control, remake, and absolutely govern men.

The supremacy of science has also meant the reinterpretation of life in terms of scientific categories. This appears, as we have seen, in the application of the mathematical concept of equality to men. The term "equality" has reference to an abstraction, and, more than that, to an abstraction of a particular variety, *quantitative abstraction*. To apply the term, as scientific political theory does, to the variety, concreteness and richness of the human situation is at once to do it a radical injustice and to

---

[11.] William Carroll Bark, *Origins of the Medieval World* (Garden City, N.Y.: Doubleday Anchor Books, 1960), 144.

introduce unrealism and injustice into the political order. Can one man equal another man, or a woman, or a tree equal a cloud? The Biblical doctrine is not equality (or inequality) but *calling,* which presupposes the necessity and value of differences. Each has his necessary place and honor and dignity in terms of his calling and his faithful discharge thereof. The idea of "a science of man" presupposes the validity of abstractions and generalizations in knowing and describing man. The Biblical faith defines man in terms of the image of God. Man has as his federal head either Adam or Christ, but, in either case, he has a vast variety of different and irreducible potentialities of calling which negate abstraction. There is unity in either Adam or in Christ, but no possible reduction to either Adam or Christ. The science of man is thus scientific mythology. The modern idea of democracy is based in part on scientific abstraction or reduction.

Seventh, because this philosophy seeks to remake man, it is hostile to the idea of punishment. Punishment assumes two things: first, responsibility on the part of the criminal, and, second, the limitation of the civil government's authority over a man to a specific and overt act of crime and to a specific, limited, and overt punishment thereof. The idea of crime as mental sickness denies limitation and places man totally in the hands of the state. As Lewis has noted, punishment is

> …always finite: you could do so much to the criminal and no more. Remedial treatment, on the other hand, need have no fixed limit; it could go on till it had effected a cure, and those who were carrying it out would decide when *that* was. And if cure were humane and desirable, how much more prevention? Soon anyone who had ever been in the hands of the police at all would come under…control…in the end, every citizen.[12]

Eighth, the French Revolution was the beginning of democracy in army service, i.e., modern conscription. Such conscription began as and is increasingly a political device serving two functions. First, it enables a state to control the populace more effectively, as well as to have an opportunity for indoctrination. Second, its purpose is to weaken and break-up as far as possible the military power in the state. In a professional army, the relationship of officers to men is a close one, and the officer both knows his troops and is able to judge their minds, morale, and potentiality. He is thus in a position, when the government is weak, to overthrow the government, because he moves in terms of an assurance in his men. A conscript army is an army of strangers, often at odds with its officers, not comparable to a professional army in strength, but safer to the state because of these things. Conscription in the modern state is thus an instrument whereby the

---

12. C. S. Lewis, *That Hideous Strength, A Modern Fairy-Tale for Grown-Ups* (New York: Collier Books, 1962), 69.

freedom of both the citizenry and the military is limited and weakened as an instrument of social control.

Ninth, in this developed and developing philosophy, foreign policy predominates over internal policy.[13] The messianic hopes of the French Revolution immediately involved it in a continuing war against the nations. The Russian Revolution is no less dedicated to this messianic faith, and the United States, which in recent years has undergone a second revolution, is equally certain of its role as world savior. Interventionism is both political and economic, and economic interventionism at home goes hand in hand historically with intervention in the affairs of foreign powers. Nothing is more clear, in a reading of the Old Testament, than the hostility of Biblical faith to this priority of foreign affairs and its concomitant, interventionism. George Washington's hostility to interventionism needs no recounting, and the Monroe Doctrine was an assertion of the immunity of the Americas from interventionism.

Tenth, humanity is the true god of the Enlightenment and of French Revolutionary thought. In all religious faiths, one of the inevitable requirements of logical thought asserts itself in a demand for *the unity of the godhead.* Hence, since humanity is god, there can be no division in this godhead, humanity. Mankind must therefore be forced to unite. Since Enlightenment philosophy is monistic, this means an intolerance of differences as unessential. National and racial differences, instead of being God-given and possessing richness and dignity to be respected, are to be obliterated. The goal is not communion but uniformity. Again, since humanity is god, the killing of any man either for crimes or in warfare is an offense. (The only permissible killing is possibly George Bernard Shaw's execution "in a kindly manner" of the enemies of socialism.) Humanistic pacifism is the result, and a pro-one-world, United Nations, peace-at-any-price faith. The godhead must be united. This faith finds expression in the U. S. Department of State Publication 7277, "Freedom From War," September, 1961.[14] This faith was expressed in the midst of war by Churchill and F. D. Roosevelt in Point 8 of the Atlantic Charter, and was ascribed to their governments: "They believe all the nations of the world, for realistic as well as spiritual reasons, must come to the abandonment of

---

[13.] See James W. Wiggins and Helmut Schoeck, eds., *Foreign Aid Reexamined* (Washington D.C.: Public Affairs Press, 1958); J. Fred Rippy, *Globe and Hemisphere* (Chicago: Regnery, 1958).

[14.] Reprinted, with introductory comments by Dr. Robert Morris, in *No Army, No Navy, No Air Force* (New York: Bookmailer, 1962). A somewhat similar view is held in *The Liberal Papers,* James Roosevelt, editor (Garden City, N.Y.: Doubleday, 1962). In these papers, armament is seen as the great problem and peace as the goal, a peace that is only the abolition of war, not a righteous order with a Godly peace. Moreover, lacking absolutes, the authors fail to see irreconcilable differences between men and nations, but only relative ones which can be bridged by aid to the enemy. See M. Stanton Evans, with Allan H. Ryskind and William Schulz, *The Fringe on Top* (New York: American Features, 1962), 204-207.

the use of force." But Scripture does not consider the legitimate use of force as an evil but rather as a necessity and a good to be used to prevent the rise and triumph of evil. Roosevelt's faith required messianic intervention with force and at the same time a condemnation of all force! Because of this coincidence of messianic interventionism and pacifism, this philosophy has created war even where men have talked most about world peace. The very idea of a United Nations *requires* war, in that it insists on irreconcilable and contradictory things. First, it insists on uniting a world and levelling all differences. Anyone with a sense of integrity must inevitably resist this levelling. Second, it seeks to create a super-state which must increasingly coerce every state, civil government, and person into line with its dream of messianic power. Third, it seeks to arrest history and freeze it into a particular mold in terms of Enlightenment thought. Inevitably, this faith is anti-Christian, and a conflict with Christianity is requisite to its being.

Eleventh, the Enlightenment, French Revolution, and proponents of modern science see *nature as eternal, infinite, and abundant*. Hence, in this tradition, as exemplified today in Marxism and welfare states, the economic problem is primarily and essentially one of *distribution, not production*. To believe in nature as created is to hold to an economy of scarcity, to an awareness of the limitations of nature and the necessity of painstaking work, i.e., production, to develop the limited means of nature. *The untouched wilderness is thus not the land of plenty, but rather the realm of plenty is free and developed civilization*, where man's labor and capital have led to productivity and a measure of cultivated abundance.

Twelfth, as we have seen, the French Revolution destroyed the remains of feudalism and federalism in France and reduced all civil government into the hands of the central power and its departments, whereas the American Revolution was the triumph of localism over centralism, and of law over majoritarianism.

Thirteenth, this philosophy, by its denial of Christianity, moved rapidly to the assumption that reality is basically *impersonal*. Hence, knowledge must be abstract and impersonal to be true, and society and man must be similarly impersonal. Dewey's hatred of personality presupposes this view of reality.[15]

Fourteenth, the state school is the established "church" and mediator of salvation to man, and children are primarily to be nurtured by and for the state.[16]

Fifteenth, as has been indicated, this philosophy is hostile to the private ownership of property. Such property as is allowed to private ownership is

---

[15.] See Rushdoony, *The Messianic Character of American Education* (Nutley, N.J.: The Craig Press, 1963).
[16.] *Ibid.*; see also Rushdoony, *Intellectual Schizophrenia: Culture, Crisis, and Education* (Phillipsburg, N.J.: Presbyterian and Reformed, 1961).

on the sufferance of the state and state planners. Implicit here is not only the priority of the state to its citizenry but also the hatred of personality in terms of an impersonal conception of ultimate reality. Moreover, the social control of man, human engineering, makes pockets of immunity to control offensive. Jeremy Bentham, an English liberal and totalitarian, wanted a model prison in which "one man would at all times be able to see the smallest movements of a thousand prisoners, and to control their most minute actions."[17] This is increasingly the dream of reason for all men.

The issues were very early stated by Burke in his *Thoughts on French Affairs,* December, 1791. According to Burke, the Reformation effected a revolution in Europe by introducing supra-national and transcendental issues and divisions into every locality, so that Europe became a system of Christian civil orders. The French Revolution introduced majoritarianism and total sovereignty. Between this Revolution and Christian Europe, no peace was possible. In his four "Letters on a Regicide Peace" a few years later, he declared that, whatever the strategic peace might be at any time, Jacobinism was a civil war against Europe as a Christian Commonwealth, and was determined on unremitting warfare against Christianity, and its "utter extirpation." Either the French Revolution and its philosophy must be destroyed, or Christian Europe eventually would be, for, "in one word, with this republic nothing independent can coexist."[18]

Time has not made that conflict more reconcilable. It has, however, seen the weakening of the American Revolution, which Burke saw as so very important to the cause of liberty. Historians are bent on seeing the American Revolution in terms of the Enlightenment, and political action today is extensively premised on French revolutionary concepts. But, since the *Communist Manifesto,* Marxism and the Communist International better express the Enlightenment and the French Revolution than does the United States, and competition between the two will work to the advantage of the more consistent system.

This mixed situation, with its conflicting presuppositions, is scarcely realized by most. Indeed, there are those who have spoken of the French Revolution as Christian or Puritan in nature! Thus, Brinton sees the values of the French Revolution as "mostly the traditional Christian, and especially Protestant Christian, virtues," and, more specifically, as "Puritan."[19] But his definition of this Puritanism is precisely the *moralism* against which the Reformation and Puritanism waged warfare, and which John Cotton, in *Revelation 13,* saw as the mark of the beast. Failure to

---

[17.] Drucker, 230.

[18.] Ross J. S. Hoffman and Paul Levack, eds., *Burke's Politics, Selected Writings and Speeches of Edmund Burke, on Reform, Revolution, and War* (New York: Alfred A. Knopf, 1949), 473.

[19.] Clarence Crane Brinton, *The Jacobins, An Essay on the New History* (New York: Russell and Russell, 1961), 175, 180.

understand what Christianity is will logically lead to failure to understand its antithesis.

11

Sphere Law

The idea of sphere law is basic to Christian orthodoxy and to an understanding of Western history. The concept is also termed sphere sovereignty, not an altogether accurate designation, since sovereignty is not ascribed to the spheres but to God and His law. Moreover, the term sphere sovereignty is a modern one, owing its central philosophical formulation to Abraham Kuyper and its great development to Herman Dooyeweerd.[1] The historical and theological origins, however, are much older and are of vast significance to our history.

In ancient history, the Tower of Babel stands as the best witness to man's virtually universal faith.[2] The unity of life was asserted, the unity of god or gods and man, of divine and human, so that man's total life, religious and political, was under the power of this unified divine-human order, against which there was no appeal. Either the ruler or king was divine, or his office carried divinity, or else divinity resided in the polis or state. There was thus no true transcendence, no appeal beyond the state and no true right beyond the state. The ancient state was a total and an absolute order, whatever its form of government. Thus of Egypt Frankfort could say, "One might say—

---

[1] For this development, see Abraham Kuyper, *Lectures on Calvinism* (Grand Rapids, Mich.: Eerdmans, 1961); Evan Runner in *Christian Perspectives 1961* (Hamilton, Ontario: Guardian Publishing Co., 1961), 188; Herman Dooyeweerd, *New Critique of Theoretical Thought* (Philadelphia: Presbyterian and Reformed, 1953-1958), 4v.

[2] See Eric Burroughs, "Some Cosmological Patterns in Babylonian Religion," in S. H. Hooke, ed., *The Labyrinth, Further Studies in the Relation between Myth and Ritual in the Ancient World* (London: SPCK, 1935), 43-70; and Andre Parrot, *The Tower of Babel* (New York: Philosophical Library, 1955).

though only metaphorically—that the community has sacrificed all freedom in order to acquire this certainty of harmony with the Gods."[3]

The sole exception to this was ancient Israel when faithful to the Lord. The priestly and kingly offices were strictly separated, although without separating religious responsibilities from the king. The rejection of Saul began with his assumption of priestly power (1 Samuel 13:9-14), and Uzziah, daring to assume like powers within the very temple, was smitten with leprosy and driven out (2 Chronicles 26:16-23). In apostasy, the state sought this union of powers in pagan cults. This unity, however, was forbidden to the human order; only in the Messiah were the priestly and royal offices, common to pagan monarchs, to be united. The development of Judaism, however, represented the apotheosis of this unity, so that, as Christ, representing the incarnation and transcendental focus of this unity, came onto the scene, he clashed at once with a hierarchy which saw the challenge of his presence. The hope of the Jews had become a world order governed by themselves as God's chosen people, with the Messiah, where accepted by a particular party within the state, seen as subservient to this hope. Christ, by refusing to make his kingdom this-worldly, i.e., to establish its center and unity in any human kingdom rather than in God, spelled death, as Caiaphas clearly saw, to the Sanhedrin's hope (John 11:49, 50). For this betrayal of its faith, Jerusalem was sentenced to destruction, and identified in Revelation 11:8 with both Sodom and Egypt.

The coming of Christ was thus a challenge to the truly totalitarian world of antiquity. The Caesars recognized the challenge and fought it savagely and bitterly, and lost.[4] With Athanasius and Augustine, the faith triumphed that there can be *no confusion* between the human and the divine orders. The created and human order is now fallen and sinful, and, even in paradise, and in the state of grace and redemption, is still creaturely. Hence, it is *limited* and *under God's absolute law.* Thus, man was freed from man's own tyranny, from the total state, and given a charter of liberty in God's word and an absolute justice in His throne.

The history of the Christian era has been largely the struggle in some sense to reestablish the divine and unitary state, the Tower of Babel bond of heaven and earth, as against the Christian sundering of that bond. One such major attempt to recreate the divine and omnipotent state was the Byzantine iconoclastic controversy, 724-843. Iconoclasm was an attack on the government of Christ, the church, by emperors of heretical leanings who sought to be sacred emperors. "I am King and Priest," Leo III wrote to

---

[3] Henri Frankfort, *Ancient Egyptian Religion* (New York: Harper, 1961), 58. See also Frankfort, *Kingship and the Gods* (Chicago: University of Chicago Press, 1948); Fustel de Coulanges, *The Ancient City* (Garden City, N.Y.: Doubleday Anchor Books, 1956); Margaret Murray, *The Divine King in England* (London: Faber and Faber).

[4] Ethelbert Stauffer, *Christ and the Caesars* (Philadelphia: Westminster, 1955).

Pope Gregory II. The empire was "to be the material form of Christendom in the terrestrial world; the Church would be only the liturgical function of the empire."[5]

In the West, the Holy Roman Empire quickly developed the same claim to represent total order, and its *one-power* theory led it to claim "apostolic" rights over the church. Against this, in terms of the Christian faith, there was the bulwark of Augustinian and Gelasian affirmations of the *two-power* theory, i.e., church and state, both under God. Later, however, Pope Innocent III abandoned this concept in favor of the *one-power* idea, the church as the divine-human bond of heaven and earth, *the* Kingdom of God on earth, embracing all institutions and governing them. *Vicarius Dei*, title of the Western emperor, has been since Innocent III an official title of the pope. This assertion led in part to the crisis of the medieval order and its collapse. Since then, Roman Catholic thought has been turning again to the Gelasian formula, of which John Courtney Murray's *We Hold These Truths* gives evidence.[6]

Meanwhile, various factors within the church paved the way for the development of sphere law and the integrity of creaturely activity. In the sixth century, Benedict's work developed the spiritual value of manual labor; this world of matter and work therein became proper areas of the Kingdom of God. With Cassiodorus, scholarship was made an area of conquest by the Kingdom. In the tenth and eleventh centuries, separation of the church from feudal subordination was a major advance in the freedom of the church. This movement had a twofold aspect. First, the Cluniac Reform, instituted in a sense by Duke William of Aquitaine, separated the religious houses from feudal control, and, second, Gregory VII separated the secular clergy from feudal ties by insisting on celibacy. The result was the further development of the integrity of the church sphere. In the thirteenth century, the church, in the Dominican and Franciscan movements, moved further into the world and into the universities. Francis in particular established a Third Order, the first two being the friars and the Poor Clares. These, the Tertiaries, lived with their families, worked in the trades, and professed their religious vocation in terms of the common life. The Friends of God and the Brethren of the Common Life are two instances of this kind of vocation.

The Reformation, while challenging the one-power concept of Innocentine faith, and of the state, was also a continuation of the new sense of priesthood being developed by the Tertiaries. Significantly, also,

---

[5.] Gerhart B. Ladner, "Origin and Significance of the Byzantine Iconoclastic Controversy," *Mediaeval Studies*, vol. II (New York: Sheed and Ward, 1940), 135.

[6.] For an excellent statement of the Roman Catholic position, see Joseph Lecler, S.J., *The Two Sovereignties, A Study of the Relationship Between Church and State* (London: Burns, Oates and Washbourne, 1952).

Augustine was a major influence on both Luther and Calvin. With respect to sphere law, Calvin at three major points fashioned the doctrines of a new world order:

1. Calvinism denied that the Kingdom of God is to be equated with the church. Instead, wherever God reigns, there is the Kingdom—and God should reign everywhere. Hence, man can serve God everywhere, and the Kingdom of God includes every area of life, and every institution which obeys His commandments. Thus, church, civil government, school, agriculture, art, business, *every realm* under God's law is an area of Kingdom activity.

2. Calvinism, both in terms of this concept of the Kingdom and in terms especially of justification by faith, which relates man directly to God, asserted the priesthood of all believers. Thus, man is as fully a priest of God at his business desk and cobbler's bench, when he faithfully obeys God, as is any ordained man in the pulpit. He has direct access to God, and serves God everywhere. Hence, the glory of the closed church meant for Protestantism that the institution and building were there for worship, but not needed for access constantly to God, who heard men everywhere. Every *sphere* of life is an area of priesthood and a place of nearness to God. Similarly, man under God is king or vice-gerent of creation, called to exercise dominion over creation by Godly exploitation, exploration, knowledge, and activity. Again, he is a prophet, called upon to interpret creation in terms of the word of God.

3. This led to a third factor, not immediately recognized but steadily asserting itself. In view of this doctrine of the spheres, and the Kingdom, *neither church nor state* has any right to rule over the spheres, since each is directly under God and equally in the Kingdom. It is Christ who is the mediator, and the only mediator, and no institution, order, or person can interfere between God and man. *Interventionism* is a pretension to deity, a claim to powers of mediation and to divine government, and hence is inadmissible.

Medieval feudalism, whatever its weaknesses, still had the Christian virtue of asserting against total government the *limitation of powers* and the responsible, contractual or feudal nature of power. It was thus a forerunner of true federalism. To this inheritance was added the Protestant concept. The independence of the spheres was an interdependence in life and activity but an independence in terms of human authority. It meant for society a necessary division of powers in institutional and sphere activity: in civil government (as developed in the United States, executive, legislative, and judicial branches, all under a constitution which presupposes a higher law), in the church (minister, session or board, members, church synods and conferences, creeds, Bible), in education (the development in the United

States of trustees, a new concept and derived from church lay rule), and in other realms a like division. Man, being a sinner, needs checks and balances. Man, being in the Kingdom and a priest, serves God everywhere. Every area has its own law-sphere, and every area its own powers as well as God-imposed restraints on its powers. Thus, physiologically, water is a fish's law-sphere, and air is man's law-sphere. A man's life involves a number of law-spheres, each with its own integrity. As he eats and digests, breathes, works, worships, functions as a citizen, and moves from sphere to sphere, he moves also from one law-realm to another, over and over through the course of a day. His activities, physical, economic, political, religious, and educational, involve him in numerous law-spheres moreover, which are both independent, in that physiology and its laws do not govern nor are they governed by mathematics, but also interdependent, in that no sphere is more than an aspect of the wholeness of created reality. Moreover, the unity of these activities and spheres is not in any one of them, in man, or in the whole, but is transcendental; it is in God only. Man experiences the spheres as unity, but he sins if he seeks to unify them under his government. Thus, no institution or sphere, nor man himself, individually or collectively, can claim to be the source or the mediator of unity and authority. Totalitarianism, civil or ecclesiastical, claims institutional divinity and authority. Scientism and rationalism claim a like power for particular kinds of intellectual activity. Anarchism, political or economic, claims it for man as the new god and final authority. Against all this, Biblical Christian faith asserts the sovereignty of God and the absolute authority of His law.

The sources of American liberty are deeply rooted in this faith and cannot long survive apart from it. The U. S. Constitution had a severe conception of the limitation of powers, and most present federal activity is in violation of the express power doctrine of the Constitution. Instead of being rootless, American history is deeply rooted and hence hostile to the empty forms of traditionalism. Its emphasis on localism and development within context are aspects of this respect for sphere law, or, from a theological point of view, for the priesthood of all believers. It has led to the great expectations which have characterized so many European views of the United States, well summarized in one French Dominican's recent expression of it: "Either America is the hope of the world or it is nothing."[7] But the hope of the world can never be reduced to a nation; it is transcendental also. And it rests, not in majorities, but in God, and in Him alone. In the dark days of the Revolutionary War, Josiah Hodgkins, a shoemaker from Ipswich, Massachusetts, serving as a company officer in Washington's army, wrote on November 25, 1775, to his wife: "There

---

[7.] R. L. Bruckberger, *Image of America* (New York: Viking, 1959), 7.

seams to be a grate Probability of a Movement Very soon But whare I can not tell. But I hope we shall Be on our garde. But our army is Very thin now But in good spirits and I hope we shall Be asisted By him houe is able with a small number to Put thousands to flite."[8] Malin has observed, with respect to historical scholarship, that, "Necessarily, even by denial, it cannot escape a religious commitment. Scholarship is sui generis."[9] If this is true of historiography, how much more true of history! History cannot escape a religious commitment nor rise above its cultural presuppositions.

[8] Herbert T. Wade and Robert A. Lively, *This Glorious Cause, The Adventures of Two Company Officers in Washington's Army* (Princeton, N.J.: Princeton University Press, 1958), 185.
[9] James C. Malin, *On the Nature of History, Essays about History and Dissidence* (Ann Arbor, Mich: J.W. Edwards, 1954), iv.

12

American Anti-Universalism

Roland Van Zandt, in his study of the philosophical premises of Jeffersonian thought, has called attention to its hostility to realism and its consistent nominalism.[1] The more basic American perspective, however, gave place to both universals and particulars and was rooted in trinitarian Christian faith rather than philosophical tradition. It was accordingly hostile to any immanent resolution in favor of either universals or particulars. It saw the resolution and reconciliation of all things in the triune God.

As a result, there was very early a development of what came to be called the New England Way, which, with equal justice, gradually came to be known as the American Way, an approach to the spheres and structures of man's life which marked a major development in Christian thought.

John Cotton spelled out its implications very early in his sermons, 1639-1650, on the thirteenth chapter of Revelation. Cotton's thesis, while having deep medieval roots and Reformation assumptions, was both a development of these inheritances and a break with them. The sermons are thus implicitly or explicitly hostile to the European churches and their establishments, to Rome very markedly, but to the Protestant churches quite strongly. Indeed, Cotton went so far as to assert that, but for the alertness on either side of the Jesuits and the Puritans, the two branches of Western Christianity could easily be reconciled.[2]

---

[1] Roland Van Zandt, *The Metaphysical Foundations of American History* (Gravenhage, Netherlands: Mouton, 1959).

[2] John Cotton, *An Exposition upon the Thirteenth Chapter of Revelation* (London, 1655), 144f.

The central premise of Cotton's position, and the New England Way, was easily stated: "We believe the Catholick Church is invisible; we believe no visible Church, but Congregations."[3] For Cotton, the beasts of Revelation 13 represented a visible world state and a visible world church, and both were anathema to him. The implications of this position are far-reaching. First of all, it is anti-perfectionist. Since the Puritans were charged with religious perfectionism very early, as their name indicates,[4] and of late with social perfectionism by Voegelin, this point needs to be stressed. They strove for a Godly order; they denied the possibility of a *perfect* order. Any civil or ecclesiastical government that claimed to embody in itself the Kingdom of God, to be *the* visible and universal order of man's life, was thereby revealing itself as the beast of the apocalypse. Second, the New England Way, as Cotton so clearly stated it, was anti-universalist. It was hostile to a one-world order in any sphere or over any sphere of life. This was not nominalism, nor was it realism; life was full of many instances of unity and plurality. No institution or order, however, could justly claim to embody within itself the unity and plurality of life. Such a catholicity and universality was transcendental and reserved to the triune God alone.

The doctrine of covenants, previously discussed, was of course basic to Cotton's thought also.[5] Since the covenants were separate law-spheres under God, no legitimate intervention by one sphere in another could be made. Ecclesiastical excommunication cannot be made civil without tyranny. The civil and ecclesiastical spheres are coordinate but distinct, and in that sense separate. False power is like the leprosy of Naaman, a disease clinging to those who lust for it. Universality is a usurpation, a denial of covenantalism and of law-spheres. As Cotton stated it, with sharpness and clarity, "It is a marvellous deliverance that God hath wrought for us in taking our religion from universality, and from outward prosperity." This rejection of universality was based on the doctrine of man. Man is a creature under God the Creator. Both by the fact of creaturehood and the further fact of man's fall, man's position is characterized by limitations. The Godly order means limited powers and limited liberty. Sinful men and sinful institutions seek to destroy these limits. The tethered beast "knows the length of his tether by morning."[6] Both true power and true liberty can only be grounded on Scripture. Power, moreover, is *ministerial,* not *legislative.* In church or state, it is the man of sin, anti-Christ, who seeks to

---

3. *Ibid.,* 13.
4. The term *Puritan* had a history as a term of reproach. It was applied in the Middle Ages to a major group, who accordingly came to be known as the *Cathari* or pure ones.
5. See Cotton's *The Covenant of God's Free Grace,* 1645, and *A Treatise of the Covenant of Grace,* 1659.
6. Cotton, *Exposition Upon the Thirteenth Chapter of Revelation,* 31f., 58, 71ff., 77.

be legislative, i.e., the creative and original source of law. In *Moses his Judicials*, Cotton observed, "The more any Law smells of man the more unprofitable."[7]

According to this perspective, man's goal cannot be the *good society* but must be a *Godly society* and a *restrained* and *restraining* government, since man is a sinner. The Garden of Eden, Paradise, was the *perfect* society, but man as sinner thrives best in terms of Godliness in the restraining government required by a sinful society. Man is barred from a return to Eden: he cannot reenter Paradise nor attempt to recreate it. Godliness and not Paradise must be his objective. Cotton warned against the offer of a good society: the offer of the "protection of a good society," he declared, "is but the smell of a Leopard."[8]

Thus Christian civil government for Cotton meant, among other things, three things certainly. First, it meant limited power; second, limited liberty; third, no universality, and no intervention by civil government into other spheres. By way of contrast, the modern messianic state aims at a self-contradiction. First, it grasps at unlimited power; second, it promises unlimited liberty, a manifest absurdity. Third, it claims increasingly a universality of jurisdiction, and the United Nations is the epitome of this tendency. It might be added that the modern concept of academic freedom similarly grasps at unlimited liberty and power within its realm.

Ziff has described the concept of government as expounded by Cotton:

> The best form was theocracy, which for Cotton meant separate but parallel civil and ecclesiastical organizations framed on the evidence of scriptures. Church and state, he believed, were of the same genus, "order," with the same author, "God," the same subject, "man," and the same end, "God's glory."

> On the level of species, however, the two diverged. Here the end of the church was the salvation of souls while that of the state was the preservation of society in justice. This meant that the subject of the church was inward man and was limited to those only who were in a state of grace, although the government, in order to preserve society, saw to it that outward man, ungodly as well as godly, attended the church meetings. Moving along parallel lines, church and state could avoid dissolving into one another by not delivering spiritual power into the hands of the magistrates, not, for instance, allowing the civil authorities to excommunicate from the church, and, conversely, by not holding a man responsible in church for his civil opinions, which procedure would bring about a type of papal excommunication. However, if the lines were not to dissolve into one another neither

---

[7.] George Lee Haskins, *Law and Authority in Early Massachusetts* (New York: Macmillan, 1960), 160.
[8.] Cotton, 20f.

were they to diverge through the failure of one to lend full and sympathetic support to the other. [9]

It was thus apparent that the New England Way, with its anti-universalism and non-interventionism, was in essence that which came to be known subsequently as the American Way. Cotton's exposition of it was theoretical, but it was also in a sense descriptive. New England was already developing the anti-universal society Cotton expounded, and he could thank God for it as "a marvellous deliverance."

[9.] Larzer Ziff, *The Career of John Cotton, Puritanism and the American Experience* (Princeton, N.J.: Princeton University Press, 1962), 97f.

13

Non-Interventionism as a Constitutional Principle

The Constitution of the United States is very clearly a non-interventionist document. The non-interventionist premise is apparent, not only in its various articles, but also in the doctrine of *express powers*. Whatever the Supreme Court interpretations of the Constitution may be, it is clear that the intention of the framers, and the language of the document itself, is the language of express powers.

Let us examine, specifically and briefly, some of these aspects of non-interventionism. First of all, Amendment IX reenforces this already implicit concept by explicitly prohibiting federal intervention in the self-government of the people. The premise of this is a concept of government very different from that prevalent today. Government is primarily self-government, and the civil order is but one form of government among the many, which includes family, church, school, society, and voluntary associations.

Second, intervention in the self-government of the states and, by implication, of their constituent units, the counties, is forbidden in Amendment X. Accordingly, internal improvements were long considered unconstitutional by many presidents and legislators. Amendment XIV has been used to nullify this concept, but the original intent and the language of that amendment were not so construed. The current welfare economy is of course interventionist in essence and alien to this constitutional provision.

Third, intervention in foreign affairs, decried by Washington in his Farewell Address, was limited by the Constitution. Article 1, Section 8, makes possible universal military conscription, but for the stated purposes only. These stated purposes are (1) to execute the laws of the Union, (2) to suppress insurrections, and (3) to repel invasions. Conscripted men thus could not be used in foreign wars, and, until 1917, this was the law of the land. This provision was rendered a nullity by the actions of Wilson and the Supreme Court.[1] Nonetheless, if the Constitution be regarded as authoritative, the burden of illegality with respect to subsequent foreign policy rests on the federal government.

Non-interventionism was thus, as we have seen, a constitutional provision with respect to persons, states, and foreign wars. It was, fourth, a principle with respect to religious policy, Amendment I being designed to prevent the intervention of the federal union into religious matters, either to establish a federal policy or to interfere in state practices.

Fifth, non-intervention with respect to money was imposed on the states as well as the federal union in Article 1, Sections 8 and 10. The premise of Andrew Jackson's constitutional struggle against the second U. S. Bank was this belief. Since the Civil War, and especially since the establishment of the Federal Reserve System, this principle has been bypassed. The Constitution had been opposed, before ratification, as a hard-money document. Its opponents saw clearly that paper money had no legal standing or lawful place under it.[2]

Sixth, the Monroe Doctrine, December 2, 1823, made two fundamental applications of this principle of non-interventionism: (1) the non-intervention by foreign powers in the Americas, and (2) non-intervention by the United States in the affairs of Europe. Both aspects are now bypassed.

Seventh, the Polk Doctrine, announced on December 2, 1845, developed this principle further by means of a three-point platform:

> 1. The people of *this continent* alone have the right to decide their own destiny.
>
> 2. We can never consent that European powers shall interfere to prevent such a union (of an independent state with the U.S.) because it might disturb the "balance of power" which they may desire to maintain upon this continent.
>
> 3. No future European colony or dominion shall with our consent be planted on any part of the North American continent.[3]

[1.] John W. Burgess, *Recent Changes in American Constitutional Theory* (New York: Columbia University Press, 1933), 59ff.

[2.] George Bancroft, *History of the Formation of the Constitution of the United States of America*, vol. II (New York: Appleton, 1882), 132, 291, 313, 380, 408.

[3.] James D. Richardson, ed., *A Compilation of the Messages and Papers of the Presidents*, vol. IV (Washington, 1904), 398f; see also Richard B. Morris, ed., *Encyclopedia of American History*, rev. ed. (New York: Harper, 1961), 192f.

Since the Russo-Japanese War, however, the U. S. has been extensively involved in balance of power politics.

Eighth, interventionism with respect to property has become the rule rather than the exception. In various ways, and by many federal agencies, property is subjected to federal intervention on a daily basis. One such instance is urban renewal. The Fifth Amendment declares: "No person shall be … deprived of … property … without due process of law, nor shall private property be taken for public use, without just compensation." Urban renewal condemns private property for private use. In 1954, in *Berman v. Parker,* the Supreme Court made this possible by ruling: "The concept of the public welfare is broad and inclusive….The values it represents are spiritual as well as physical, esthetic as well as monetary." Urban renewal, by taking property from some for the profit of others, has thus been conducive to the oligarchic development which the founding fathers feared.

The basis of this change from non-interventionism to interventionism in constitutional theory is a sociological approach to the Constitution. Its original intent is supplanted by present demands. As Kik has observed, "The Supreme Court is limited to the intent of those who composed the First Amendment. Otherwise, we are no longer under a *constitutional* government."[4] In terms of this new mode of interpretation, it has been repeatedly noted, we are less and less under the Constitution and increasingly under the Supreme Court.

The roots of this trend must be sought, however, elsewhere than in the Supreme Court, which to a large extent mirrors a cultural phenomenon. Its origins are religious. Even as the origins of the republic were in Christian faith, so its decline is rooted in developments within the life of the Church. In the past century, churches have steadily developed a principle of interpretation which, not surprisingly, has taken root in society at large, and in the courts. The Bible and the various creeds have been interpreted, not in terms of their original intent, but in terms of contemporary science, politics, economics, and cultural mores. The original meaning has been clearly suppressed or bypassed to make way for modern requirements. Instead of dropping the Creed or Bible, its authority has been used to justify new contents by means of interpretation. The conclusion is a simple one: if men deal so with the things of God, why not so with the Constitution? Is there, then, cause for complaint if the Supreme Court applies modern religious methodology to law? The issue thus is basically a loss of character as a consequence of a loss of faith. The Constitution still stands, basically the same document despite certain amendments, and its character has

---

4. J. Marcellus Kik, *The Supreme Court and Prayer in the Public School* (Philadelphia: Presbyterian and Reformed, 1963), 27. See David Leslie Hoggan, *Conflict in 1937: The Supreme Court, The Federal System, and the Constitution;* soon to be published.

changed little in the past fifty years. The interpretation thereof has changed, reflecting a now deeply rooted revolution in American faith and life. The outcome of the struggle between the older faith and the newer approach will certainly be reflected at the polls and in the courts, but it will be settled first of all in the religious decisions of men. Inescapably, history is the outworking of religious commitments.

Appendix

Suggested
Additional Reading

The following reading list is limited to studies more likely to be of interest to the general reader. The footnotes can be consulted for further references.

Baldwin, Alice M.: *The New England Clergy and the American Revolution.* New York: Ungar, 1958. First published in 1928, this study analyzes the clergy's teaching of Biblical political science and traces its influence on the Revolution.

Becker, Carl L.: *The Declaration of Independence, A Study in the History of Political Ideas.* New York: Vintage, 1958. Presuppositions of the Declaration analyzed.

Benton, Thomas Hart: *Thirty Years' View.* New York: Appleton, 1854, 2 vols. Bulky, but excellent for insight into the important years, 1820-1850.

Bredvold, Louis I.: *The Brave New World of the Enlightenment.* Ann Arbor: University of Michigan Press, 1961. Delightful and long-overdue analysis of the Enlightenment; necessary reading.

Bridenbaugh, Carl: *Mitre and Sceptre, Transatlantic Faiths, Ideas, Personalities, and Politics, 1689-1775.* New York: Oxford University Press, 1962. Religion as a fundamental cause of the Revolution.

Brown, Robert E.: *Charles Beard and the Constitution.* Princeton, N. J.: Princeton University Press, 1956. A critical analysis of Beard's *An Economic Interpretation of the Constitution.*

Burgess, John W.: *Recent Changes in American Constitutional Theory* (1923). New York: Columbia University Press, 1933. Important look at the period from 1898 onward. Burgess did not deal with the constitutional consequences of the Civil War in this work, nor did he consider them dangerous.

Cooper, James Fenimore: *The American Democrat.* New York: Vintage, 1956. A classic which continues to be very useful in understanding many aspects of life in the young republic.

Corwin, Edward S.: *The "Higher Law" Background of American Constitutional Law* (1928). Ithaca, N.Y.: Cornell University Press, 1955. Relation of transcendental and natural law to Constitution.

Coulter, E. Merton: *The South During Reconstruction, 1865-1877.* Baton Rouge: Louisiana State University Press, 1947.

Covey, Cyclone: *The American Pilgrimage, The Roots of American History, Religion and Culture.* New York: Collier, 1961. Study of the religious origins of American culture. Brilliant analysis, but sees Platonism too far back in Puritanism.

De Tocqueville, Alexis: *Democracy in America,* 2 vols. New York: Langley, 1841. Invaluable perspective on the American character and culture of the day. Should be read in an unabridged text.

Hall, Thomas Cuming: *The Religious Background of American Culture.* Boston: Little, Brown, 1930. Much criticized and much admired study, tracing American culture to Wyclif and Lollards as sources of the dissenting tradition.

Hall, Verna, etc., eds.: *Christian History of the Constitution of the United States,* vols. 1-3. San Francisco: American Christian Constitution Press, 1960, 1962, 1964. Collections of documents and historical writings; vol. 3 especially important.

Haraszti, Zoltan: *John Adams and the Prophets of Progress.* Cambridge: Mass.: Harvard University Press, 1952. Collection of Adams' marginal notes to works of European *philosophes.* Excellent on Adams, and especially delightful reading.

Haskins, George Lee: *Law and Authority in Early Massachusetts, A Study in Tradition and Design.* New York: Macmillan, 1960. A very readable first volume in the study of early Massachusetts law. This series may well become one of the major works in colonial history.

Kuyper, Abraham: *Lectures on Calvinism* (1931). Grand Rapids, Mich.: Eerdmans, 1961. Calvinism and sphere law presented in summary fashion. The Princeton Stone Lectures for 1898.

Kik, J. Marcellus: *The Supreme Court and Prayer in the Public School.* Philadelphia: Presbyterian and Reformed, 1963. Valuable not only with respect to the issue discussed but as a study in an aspect of constitutionalism.

Kilpatrick, James Jackson: *The Sovereign States, Notes of a Citizen of Virginia.* Chicago: Regnery, 1957. The modern argument for states' rights and its historical foundations, carefully and ably presented.

Kraus, Michael: *A History of American History.* New York: Farrar and Rinehart, 1937. Much of what we believe to be history is the interpretation of historians; this fact needs study. Kraus' book does not do justice to many historians but is a start in the study of the problem. Far better are the works of James C. Malin; see especially his *Essays on Historiography* (1953), *On the Nature of History* (1954), *Confounded Rot About Napoleon* (1961), and *The Nebraska Question, 1852-1854* (1953), published by author, Lawrence, Kansas. For the general reader, Malin is not easy reading, but he is one of the most rewarding of American historians.

McDonald, Forrest: *We the People, Economic Origins of the Constitution.* Chicago: University of Chicago Press, 1958. Thorough dissection of Beard's economic determinism.

McIlwaine, Charles Howard: *The American Revolution: A Constitutional Interpretation* (1923). Ithaca, N.Y.: Cornell University Press, 1961. Ably demonstrates that colonial theory was not Whig philosophy.

McLaughlin, Andrew C.: *Foundations of American Constitutionalism* (1932). New York: Fawcett, 1961. The influence of New England ideas and principles on American constitutionalism.

Metzger, Charles H., S.J.: *Catholics and the American Revolution, A Study in Religious Climate.* Chicago: Loyola University Press, 1962. Catholic perspective on the Protestant nature of the Revolution.

Miller, Perry: *The American Puritans, Their Prose and Poetry.* Garden City, N.Y.: Doubleday Anchor, 1956.
— *Errand into the Wilderness.* Cambridge: Belknap, 1956.
— *The New England Mind, From Colony to Province.* Cambridge, Mass.: Harvard University Press, 1962. *The New England Mind, The Seventeenth Century.* New York: Macmillan, 1939.
— *Orthodoxy in Massachusetts, 1630-1650, A Genetic Study.* Cambridge, Mass.: Harvard University Press, 1933.
Miller's works place his readers in his debt. His lack of theological perspective sometimes limits his awareness of issues.

Niebuhr, H. Richard: *The Kingdom of God in America.* Chicago: Willett, Clark, 1937. Able analysis of the meaning of American Christianity and its conception of what constitutes true society. Important to an understanding of American history.

Painter, Sidney: *Feudalism and Liberty, Articles and Addresses.* Ed. by Fred A. Cazel Jr. Baltimore: Johns Hopkins Press, 1961. Latter articles deal with thesis of title. More work needed in this area.

Pollard, A. F.: *Factors in American History.* Cambridge: University Press, 1925. An excellent study by an English scholar, who writes on American history and its significance with insight and knowledge.

Schneider, Herbert W.: *The Puritan Mind* (1930). Ann Arbor, Mich.: Anchor Paperback, 1958. Good introduction to and commentary on the Puritan mind. Much is made of the loss of a sense of sin, but what is first needed is a careful study of what constituted the Puritan sense of sin.

Smith, Chard Powers: *Yankees and God.* New York: Hermitage, 1954. Study of Puritanism and its influence on U.S. Sometimes too general, often stimulating.

Stevens, C. Ellis: *Sources of the Constitution of the United States, Considered in Relation to Colonial and English History.* New York: Macmillan, 1894. Study of the political inheritance.

Stryker, Lloyd Paul: *Andrew Johnson, A Study in Courage.* New York: Macmillan, 1929. An important study of a great and neglected president.

Van Wagenen Jr., Jared: *The Golden Age of Homespun.* Ithaca, N.Y.: Cornell University Press, 1953. A highly readable and realistic account of the homespun era.

Webster, Nesta H.: *The French Revolution, A Study in Democracy,* London: Constable, 1921. Very important in understanding the nature of the French Revolution, rooted in the Enlightenment, in order to assess the difference from the American Revolution.

Woodhouse, A.S.P., ed.: *Puritanism and Liberty, Being the Army Debates* (1647-9). London: Dent, 1938. Important in understanding the Puritan concept of liberty, and the relation of Christianity to the state.

Index

The Author

Rousas John Rushdoony (1916-2001) was a well-known American scholar, writer, and author of over thirty books. He held B.A. and M.A. degrees from the University of California and received his theological training at the Pacific School of Religion. An ordained minister, he worked as a missionary among Paiute and Shoshone Indians as well as a pastor to two California churches. He founded the Chalcedon Foundation, an educational organization devoted to research, publishing, and cogent communication of a distinctively Christian scholarship to the world at large. His writing in the *Chalcedon Report* and his numerous books spawned a generation of believers active in reconstructing the world to the glory of Jesus Christ. He resided in Vallecito, California until his death, where he engaged in research, lecturing, and assisting others in developing programs to put the Christian Faith into action.

The Ministry of Chalcedon

CHALCEDON (kal•see•don) is a Christian educational organization devoted exclusively to research, publishing, and cogent communication of a distinctively Christian scholarship to the world at large. It makes available a variety of services and programs, all geared to the needs of interested ministers, scholars, and laymen who understand the propositions that Jesus Christ speaks to the mind as well as the heart, and that His claims extend beyond the narrow confines of the various institutional churches. We exist in order to support the efforts of all orthodox denominations and churches. Chalcedon derives its name from the great ecclesiastical Council of Chalcedon (A.D. 451), which produced the crucial Christological definition: "Therefore, following the holy Fathers, we all with one accord teach men to acknowledge one and the same Son, our Lord Jesus Christ, at once complete in Godhead and complete in manhood, truly God and truly man...." This formula directly challenges every false claim of divinity by any human institution: state, church, cult, school, or human assembly. Christ alone is both God and man, the unique link between heaven and earth. All human power is therefore derivative: Christ alone can announce that "All power is given unto me in heaven and in earth" (Matthew 28:18). Historically, the Chalcedonian creed is therefore the foundation of Western liberty, for it sets limits on all authoritarian human institutions by acknowledging the validity of the claims of the One who is the source of true human freedom (Galatians 5:1).

The *Chalcedon Report* is published monthly and is sent to all who request it. All gifts to Chalcedon are tax deductible.

Chalcedon
Box 158
Vallecito, CA 95251 U.S.A.
www.chalcedon.edu

Printed in the USA
CPSIA information can be obtained
at www.ICGtesting.com
CBHW021911180824
13384CB00006B/52